What Business
Unlocking I

MW00945012

"Do Better Projects and Do ̲̲̲̲̲̲̲̲̲ increase the velocity of new ̲̲̲̲̲̲̲̲̲ ̲̲̲̲̲̲̲̲̲ ̲̲̲̲̲̲̲̲̲ ̲̲̲̲̲̲̲̲̲ ̲̲̲̲̲̲̲̲̲ ̲̲̲̲̲̲̲̲̲ growth for any company. Thankfully, Dalton provides the critical ingre-dients for that recipe to set your organization up to successfully drive needed change. This book is easy to read and more importantly, easy to apply as he coaches and guides you through the process. Highly Recom-mended!"

— Sean Craig, Global VP Product Management and R&D
–Maxcess International

"As engaging as any novel; internalizing Mike's simple but insightful con-cepts will definitely result in shortening your NPD cycle and maximizing the value of your innovation portfolio."

— Asim Syed, Director, Global Technical Service R&D
—Dow AgroSciences

"I had the pleasure to implement a new way of working in our organiza-tion together with Mike. The results speak for themselves–we have im-proved our project throughput remarkably without adding more re-sources. This book very nicely illustrates the process we have been through, step by step. Definitely worth reading–either before or during the change management process you intend to take your organization through."

– Luise Bang, Global Head of PMO – Danfoss A/S

"A deft application of Lean thinking and concepts to the NPD process—time and again, these concepts are key to improving productivity in every process."

—Darryl Nazareth, SVP Global Operations and R&D
—Ansell Healthcare

"Adroitly describes the central challenges facing project management in the New Product Development area and offers a solution set which is sim-ultaneously pragmatic and effective. The myths about project manage-ment are, in my estimation, universal - as are the nine accelerators out-lined herein. This is a must-read book for anyone serious about improv-ing New Product Development."

—Bill Flood, VP of Engineering, Advanced Technology and New
Business Ventures–Moog Aircraft Group

"Rare is the person that possesses the depth of understanding needed to "Crack the Code" on new product innovation. Rarer still is the person that can effectively teach, coach, and communicate sound solutions and practices to address this vexing business issue. Mike Dalton is that rare expert, and this book shares that expertise in a way that all business people can learn from."

— Nick Maris, President & CEO–Somna Therapeutics

"Unlocking Innovation Productivity Dalton addresses a somewhat neglected but very important topic for innovation - how to efficiently move projects through the funnel and to commercial success."
—Timothy Pratt, Chief of Staff & Chief Strategy Officer
—Applied Materials

"Dalton understands how critical innovation is to company success and provides succinct reasoning and actionable steps to overcome innovation challenges. Short and easy to read, making it perfect for any team member."

— Jim Estill, CEO–Danby Appliances

"A prescription for what ails product development in a concise integration of lean, constraints-based methods along with a career's worth of practical insight and practices."

— Joe Pfaff, VP Off-Highway Engineering—Husco International

"Distills decades' worth of new product development experience and success into deployable and easy-to-understand strategies. Mike's approach is both counterintuitive and pragmatic, offering senior executives both a sense of affirmation related to NPD struggles and a direction for a more productive future."

— Jeff Kerlin, President & CEO—Tailored Label Products

"A practical, easy to follow guide to more productive new product development. Dalton's methods are proven, and his writing style brings clarity and just the right amount of detail to the reader."

— Joe Wright, President—Concept Metals

"Masterfully challenges the traditional thinking that's holding you back with solid examples and proven results. No matter the maturity of your innovation process, you will get value from these strategies for upping your innovation game.

— Wayne Laning, VP Engineering & Quality—Bemis Manufacturing

"An easy and insightful read that shares a proven formula for driving successful Innovation. Mike expertly navigates the reader along the pathway to outstanding NPD results by leveraging Theory of Constraints and pointing out the potential pitfalls along the way."

— Doug Brown, Vice President Engineering—VSG-Dover

"A quick read for business leaders who want to see their new product and innovation results break away from the pack. Dalton emphasizes strategies and critical areas of focus which will enhance speed, reduce risk, and improve return."

— Mike Zedalis, President —Tingley Rubber Inc.

"Combines the well-established principles of lean business and Theory of Constraints with pragmatic strategies for an actionable roadmap that business leaders can use to increase project portfolios returns. A must-read for professionals at every level of the organization."

– Amit Sachdeva, Director, Product Management—Danfoss

"Mike Dalton has a deep understanding of the theory of constraints and critical chain which used in combination with his background and great communication skills has allowed him to develop an innovation process that is practical, systematic, and powerful."

— Carlos Andres Arroyave Carvajal, CEO—Colorquimica SA

"Challenges common practices for NPD project and portfolio management with a practical application of the Theory of Constraints and a fresh approach to prioritization that unlocks organizational capacity with a bias toward delivering value."

— Lisa Franklin, Director, Global Product Strategy & Portfolio Mgmt
—Johnson Controls Power Solutions

"One of the greatest signs of subject mastery is the ability to condense complexity to actionable clarity. Mike Dalton does just that with the challenge of delivering Innovation results. Rarely has 141 pages yielded so much benefit. Mike's "doing better projects/doing projects better" approach promises to maximize your commercial impact with the resources you have and transform your effort into productive effort. Isn't that what we all want? Making the most cash positive impact possible for our organizations, Unlocking Innovation Productivity offers a powerful weapon in that quest."

– Collin G. Moore, Ph.D., Director of Strategic Innovation and Open
Innovation Studio – Avery Dennison

"You don't get paid for the new products you work on. You only get paid for the new products that you successfully launch. As you read this, you are shaking your head yes – of course. But realistically, is that how your company runs its NPD process? If not, this book is for you – it delivers a framework of real-world, practical processes that will enable your team to build an effective NPD structure in your company."

– Paul Byrne, VP & GM Building Specialties
–Bradley Corporation

"Concisely articulates the root causes of product development problems along with a methodical approach for how to select the best new projects, streamline workflows, engage cross-functional teams, and build a learning organization. Ultimately, he demonstrates how his easy-to-understand improvement strategies can lead to customer value creation and profitable growth."

– Dan Glusick, VP Innovation Center & Rexnord Business Systems
–Rexnord Corporation

A Roadmap for Business and R&D Leaders Who Are Tired of Throwing More Money and People at New Product Delays

Unlocking Innovation Productivity

Proven Strategies for Making New Products a
Resilient Competitive Advantage

Michael A. Dalton

The Leading Authority on Accelerating
Predictable New Product Growth

**Flywheel
Effect**
Publishing

Copyright Revised Edition © 2021 Michael A. Dalton & Guided Innovation Group, LLC

Copyright First Edition © 2016 Michael A. Dalton & Guided Innovation Group, LLC

All rights reserved. This book or any portion thereof may not be reproduced or used in any manner whatsoever without the publisher's express written permission.

Flywheel Effect Publishing is a Division of Guided Innovation Group, LLC

Acknowledgments

To my wonderful wife, Carol, who continues to be a playful source of joy and inspiration.

To all the clients who have trusted me to advise them over the years—and especially to those that have shared that lightbulb moment and welcomed me into their worlds to help them transform their organizations.

"Three Rules of Work: Out of clutter find simplicity; From discord find harmony; In the middle of difficulty lies opportunity. **"**

—*Albert Einstein*

Table of Contents

Innovation – A Market-Driven Definition:

The Organization-Wide Capability & Passion for Finding and Profitably Serving Unmet Customer and Market Needs

Innovation Challenges

Skim through any of the current thinking on innovation in popular business media, and you'll find the focus is on creativity, ideation, and invention. But when I work with business leaders trying to drive new product growth, these rarely emerge as their core constraint.

Instead, the challenges that I hear most center on execution—the basic blocking and tackling of moving new product projects through the organization to capture windows of opportunity and deliver promised sales growth.

After many such discussions, I've seen innovation challenges narrow down to just a handful of undesirable effects regardless of industry or region.

a) **Low Project Throughput**: Simply not getting as many new products to market as you need or want
b) **Poor On-Time Performance:** Struggling to predict and commit to timelines that your business can achieve
c) **Minimal Market Impact:** Too many resources going to low-impact programs that don't deliver as promised

d) **Long Time to Market / Slow Speed to Market**: Projects taking too long causing you to miss critical windows of opportunity

e) **Not Enough Resources**: Constantly hearing that your people are stretched too thin

If any of these issues resonate for your business, that can only make growth harder than it needs to be—and more costly, too. And that last challenge can be the most frustrating of all. The tired old refrain goes something like, *"If we only had more resources..."* Because conventional thinking always says that more money and more people are the answer.

Well, I'm going to challenge that premise throughout this book—Throwing money and people at new product delays just isn't the answer!

Of course, that's what your intuition has been telling you all along—isn't it?

> **"Throwing money and people at new product delays just isn't the answer... "**

So if throwing more resources at it isn't the answer, then what is? Before answering that, you need to understand the root of these problems. But much of what I share will contradict the practices you've seen throughout your career.

There is still a grain of truth you need to confront about resources. Without a sustained improvement in productivity—a change in the status quo—your existing resources won't ever be able to get it all done.

To underscore this point, imagine for a moment a situation where, as the CEO, your head of manufacturing comes into your office and tells you that there is no way to increase productivity. "This continuous improvement thing was just a fad and has played itself out. It would just be easier to invest in more capacity."

Would I be wrong to guess that you'd be thinking about finding their replacement before they cleared your office threshold?

That's why it amazes me that so many organizations just seem to accept the current level of new product development productivity—never making the leap to driving gains in innovation with a systematic, continuous improvement-based approach.

Sure, many companies have implemented conventional tools like stage-gate processes, project lifecycle management software, or even rapid-prototyping. These can be useful, but too often, they are just part of a solution searching for a problem—one of the many solutions hacking at the branches of the problem instead of the few striking at the roots. [1]

Unless a solution systematically deals with the root causes, its impact will be minimal and unsustainable.

> **"One of the many solutions hacking at the branches of the problem instead of the few striking at the roots... "**

The Lightbulb Moment that Forever Changed my Approach to Innovation

It was nearly 15 years ago, and I was the Americas Regional Business Unit Leader for the industrial polymer division of the SC Johnson & Son family of companies. We had a strong reputation as innovators helping the printing, packaging, coatings, and adhesives markets replace harmful solvents with more environmentally friendly water-based technologies.

I had an engineering degree and an MBA. I studied everything I could get my hands on around growth strategy and new product innovation. We had gone through a very time-consuming and costly stage-gate effort, and I had personally led a transformation moving the global organization to market-driven business units.

Yet, the business continued to have the same challenges we'd always had, with projects taking longer than planned and under-delivering as a result. And no surprise, we never had enough resources—even with R&D spending topping 7% of net sales.

At about that same time, an unusual new improvement effort in our manufacturing operation caught my attention. We were starting to run short on manufacturing capacity and needed to act. Benchmarking showed that we were already one of the most efficient producers in the specialty chemicals field. Following conventional thinking, we had pretty much accepted that it was time to spend tens of millions of dollars on another emulsion reactor—an investment we had just come to expect to have to make every three to five years.

However, a team of very bright manufacturing engineers challenged that assumption. They started experimenting with a relatively new approach called the Theory of Constraints (TOC). [2] The idea was to ignore traditional local efficiency measures and instead focus on the bottleneck.

Their results were stunning. They "added" an additional reactor's worth of capacity with almost no investment in just a few months.

I was blown away! So much so that I just had to find out how they had pulled off this miracle in such a short timeframe. How could it be possible to accomplish so much so rapidly—and without extra resources or investment?

What the team had done was focus all the improvement on the bottleneck of the production system. The reactors were the bottleneck, so they ensured nothing upstream or downstream prevented the reactors from running their batches and moving on to the next as quickly as possible. They subordinated every operating decision to the productivity of those reactors.

That was the lightbulb moment that forever changed my approach to new product innovation. As I dove in to understand the concepts and learn the frameworks and tools they had used, I began to see how many of these same ideas could also drive new product innovation.

The outcome was a powerful new framework for rapidly driving productivity and predictability in new product development. It's a straightforward concept—simply put better and better opportunities into a system that subordinates everything else to moving them towards launch as quickly and predictably as possible.

Building on this approach, I eventually ventured out to help technology-based and industrial manufacturers achieve the full potential of their new product efforts—the same basic strategies that I've been using and refining ever since as the Guided Innovation System.

The first client I advised with this approach was in the industrial steam generation equipment market. Their time-to-launch had ballooned to three years, and even small projects seemed to go on forever. To some of the managers there, the steps we took to address it, like working on less to finish more, seemed counter-intuitive—maybe even a little crazy...

But it wasn't long before their most important programs started moving once again, and they soon experienced the value of focused execution. Within less than a year, they were on track to cut time-to-market in half and were eventually finishing projects in as little as ten months.

As a result, they brought more successful new products to market in the next year than they had in the previous three. They also reduced development expenses by over a million dollars since they were no longer paying for prototype services and regulatory certifications on products with little chance of ever reaching the market.

Since then, I've used these strategies to successfully coach and guide executives and their teams around the world in many different technology-intensive and industrial businesses. Including electronics; specialty chemicals; consumer products; industrial equipment; heating, air conditioning, and refrigeration; automation, flowmeters, sensors and control systems; medical products; safety products; software; and OEM components.

In the next chapter, I'll share some of the myths and conventional practices you'll have to overcome to achieve these types of gains.

Striking at the Roots

If you've read this far, the conventional "wisdom" underlying traditional project management is likely hiding 50% or more of your innovation capacity.

That's right—the tools intended to help fix the problem are actually making it worse—or at best, keeping you from making the kinds of breakthroughs that are possible.

This claim may be a lot to swallow at this point, but bear with me. Throughout this chapter, I will share some of the myths at the root of this waste. After that, I'm confident you'll see the validity of this claim for yourself.

Myth #1 – Busy Equals Productive

You've seen it before—people running from one meeting to the other with hardly enough time to catch their breath in between—much less time to think about and do the essential things needed to move your business forward.

> **"The conventional "wisdom" underlying traditional project management is hiding 50% or more of your innovation capacity... "**

When I work with companies to improve new product productivity, this is usually one of the first and most apparent behaviors I find. It's a culture that rewards activity instead of results. Being busy looks productive, but effort isn't the same as achievement.

Of course, multitasking is the holy grail for this culture and the activity junkies it breeds. It's no wonder, with pop culture exalting multitasking as a must-have skill. Many well-meaning but misguided job descriptions even include it as a requirement.

The reality is that multitasking is the ultimate proof that being busy is not the same as being productive. Hopefully, the two-minute test on the next two pages will prove that to you—and quite conclusively.

Important Note: Please don't skip this test to save the two minutes it will take you! Many executives still mention the positive impact it has had on their thinking years after taking it.

In this test, you will run two mini-projects—one without multitasking and one with it.

Let's start by timing how long it takes you to write the following two lines in sequence without multitasking. Once you start a timer, simply copy the words in Project 1 followed by the alphabet in Project 2:

Project 1:

RAPID NEW PRODUCT INNOVATIONS

Project 2:

ABCDEFGHIJKLMNOPQRSTUVWXYZ

Project 1 Duration (without multitasking):

_____

Project 2 Duration (without multitasking):

_____

It probably took you anywhere from 15-20 seconds to complete each project for a total of 30-40 seconds.

Now let's see how productive you are with multitasking. With the timer running, start by writing one letter from Project 1 on the line below, then one letter from Project 2, then back to Project 1, and so on. The sequence should look like this:

R,A,A,B,P,C,I,D,D,E,N,F.....

Project 1:

RAPID NEW PRODUCT INNOVATIONS

Project 2:

ABCDEFGHIJKLMNOPQRSTUVWXYZ

Project 1 (Duration with multitasking):

_____

Project 2 (Duration with multitasking):

_____

How long did it take you this time? Most people need between 25-40 seconds for each—50-100% longer for each project. And did you notice? With multitasking, it was at least twice as long before anything finished.

After taking the test, what kind of effect do you think this could be having on your team members' productivity?

Did you notice how uncomfortable you felt switching back and forth? The interruptions made it impossible to get into a rhythm or flow.

Also, when I run this exercise with groups, someone invariably mentions the mistakes they made. Not only did their penmanship suffer, but many missed a letter or two in the alphabet or misspelled one of the words. Multitasking hurts quality.

Humans just aren't built to multitask when it comes to knowledge work. So what you are seeing is what I call "Multitasking Overhead."

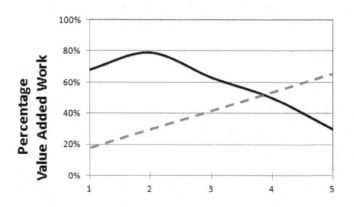

Number of Projects per Engineer

Figure 1 - Multitasking Overhead

Figure 1 shows what happened in a study where engineers had different numbers of project assignments to manage simultaneously. [3] The more projects they had to keep moving, the less value-added work they accomplished.

The act of keeping all the balls in the air or all the plates spinning became work in itself—the non-value-added overhead you see in the red line. A form of waste eating away at productivity. While often unnoticed, the accumulated effect can be quite devastating.

An important note here, though. This chart might lead you to conclude that having two things to work on is more productive. What's happening here in a conventional system is that while waiting on something for one project, the engineer can switch to another. That might feel more productive, but what if you could eliminate much of the waiting? More on that coming up in Myth #3 – You Have to Run More Projects to Get More Done.

So if multitasking has such a negative effect, why is it so pervasive? Why would anyone purposely choose to work this way?

Again, one of the answers lies in conventional project and resource management beliefs. The fallacy being that if you keep everyone busy, more work will get done—but busy doing what?

Since most businesses don't have much visibility into actual project status, busy becomes a proxy for productive. And busy is rewarded because it's easier to see. So it becomes habitual to keep too many plates spinning, jumping back and forth between them without finishing.

Additionally, project managers learn to use their influence and persuasion skills to keep their own projects moving. But that means other projects end up struggling for resources, which simply results in cascading the delays.

Making managers and their teams aware of the waste inherent in multitasking can help—for a while. But the status quo is a powerful force. You won't see lasting improvements without other changes in the way you operate, as you'll see in the coming chapters.

Myth #2 – You Finish a Project On-Time by Finishing Every Task On-Time

Have you ever said this to yourself? "If people would just do their jobs and get their tasks finished when they are supposed to, all our new products would launch on-time."

I know I have—but I've also learned that couldn't be any further from the truth. Let me show you why.

I'm not suggesting that project teams should not be committed to achieving every project by its due date. Nor am I suggesting that there shouldn't be milestones for high-level deliverables such as "First Shipment" or "Prototype Delivery."

What I am suggesting is that the project due date and those deliverable dates are the only dates that matter. Milestone and deadline thinking for the other tasks in a project just ends up extending timelines while still exposing the due date to slippage.

Still, that's how traditional project management would have us proceed—building a project plan and assigning due dates to every task. Here's an example to help you see the impact of that approach.

Let's say you had to estimate how long it would take to finish one of the tasks in a project, and that task was to go to the closest Starbucks and bring back a refreshing beverage for everyone on your team. If I asked you to guess how long it would take, what would your estimate be? The answer would depend on your assumptions.

So let's compare two trips. In the first, everything goes perfectly. You don't run into any traffic. The weather is perfect. You hit green lights the entire way, have no parking problems, and don't have to wait in line at the drive-up when you get there. Also, there are no speed traps on your way there or back. This near-perfect trip represents touch time—where everything goes smoothly with no unexpected delays.

So how long did that imaginary journey take? Since there is a Starbucks within 2 miles of anywhere in the country, or at least it seems like it, you might estimate around 20 minutes.

Then imagine a different trip where you leave your office at rush hour. It's pouring rain, you get stopped at every traffic light, and you wait in traffic because of an accident. When you get to Starbucks, the parking lot is full, and there's a long line in the drive-through. The only lucky thing about this trip is that you didn't get a speeding ticket, but mainly because you never reached the speed limit. Well, that and you weren't in an accident.

Which imaginary trip would you use for your estimate? Especially if your ability to achieve tasks on time factors into your performance review. Is there any chance that you wouldn't build some safety into your projection?

And that's what happens when people inside your organization build project plans. They add safety over and above the touch time estimate and then use those "safe" estimates to assign a required completion date for each task.

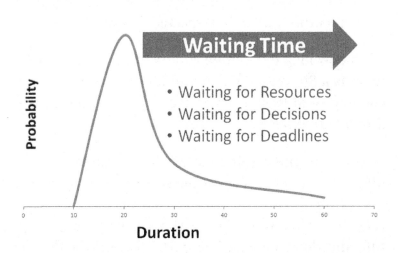

Figure 2 - Cumulative Probability of Task Duration

For our caffeinated example, Figure 2 shows that there is a 50% cumulative probability that the task will finish within 20-25 minutes. But anyone with any project savvy will give you an estimate that they can hit better than 90% of the time—so the estimate you get is closer to 40-50 minutes.

After all, they want to provide a realistic estimate, including the issues that often get in the way. That means they will add anywhere from one to two times the length of the actual work as safety against uncertainty—but what kind of uncertainty?

Well, they might run into an unexpected technical issue with the task. They might also be interrupted to work on another task for a few minutes or a few days.

After all, multitasking is a real-world issue, and your people know it.

The result is that most projects end up planned at two to three times the duration it would take solely based on the work effort.

The conventional argument goes that this safety is needed to protect against uncertainty. That makes sense on the surface. But digging a level deeper, with all that safety included, why do so many projects still finish late?

After all, if you put that added safety in each task, some will need it, but others will finish early. Shouldn't they cancel each other out?

The problem is that traditional project management puts safety in each task and gives each task its own due date. But work expands to fill the time available. That means the safety in each task encourages procrastination.

The biggest culprit is something called Student Syndrome. You no doubt experienced it when you were in school. Give a student more time than they need to write a research paper, and they wait until the last possible minute to start. Then if anything goes wrong, they either pull an all-nighter or turn it in late.

That's not to say students are lazy. They may have so many other assignments that they only worry about what's due next and simply ignore those that aren't due within the next few days.

Unfortunately, Student Syndrome isn't limited to students. It also isn't the only type of procrastination; Perfectionism and Sandbagging are two others you may face.

With Perfectionism, sometimes referred to as Apple Polishing, a researcher might finish a five-day task in only three days. But with all that safety, it's tempting to continue running a few more iterations, experiments, or tests—relentlessly pursuing perfection at the expense of an on-time launch.

Sandbagging, or unreported finishes, occurs when a team member finishes a task early but fails to report it. The primary reason this happens is that an early finish might raise the expectations for next time—even if it was a unique situation that allowed for the early finish.

In a busy environment with the actual status hidden and the task-level safety wasted on procrastination, unexpected problems inevitably derail your chances for an on-time finish. That why experienced project managers know that delays accumulate while early finishes evaporate.

> **"Delays accumulate while early finishes evaporate ... "**

Again, awareness of these behaviors is vital as a foundation, but as you'll see shortly, creating a lasting transformation takes a more holistic approach to your entire new product operating system.

Myth #3 – You Have to Run More Projects to Get More Done

Too many managers fall into the trap of believing the more projects their teams work on, the more they will get done. But once you reach the number of projects with optimal flow and project throughput, every project you add reduces the number you can complete during any given period.

The key is to realize that most companies don't get paid for the new products they work on. They only get paid for the new products that they successfully launch and start selling.

Let's look at an example applying this to your new product pipeline. Let's say you have four opportunities in front of you and:

- All 4 are for equally important customers
- If you put your entire team on 1 project, they can complete it in 3 months

- Each has the same return—$1M cashflow at the end of the quarter in which it is completed and every quarter after that
- Each project has an influential internal sponsor pushing to start immediately

Now, if you're completely honest with yourself, what are the chances that your company wouldn't spread the resources out and have people working on each one?

Figure 3 is a one-year snapshot of what it would look like to run all four simultaneously. The solid color on each horizontal line represents each project's work effort, and the un-shaded W's indicate the wait time when resources are working on other projects.

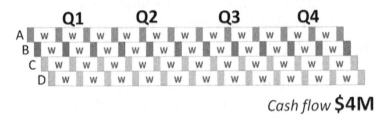

Cash flow **$4M**

Figure 3 – Simultaneous Execution

Your resources move back and forth between projects, so three-fourths of each project's timeline is waiting time. A full year later, at the end of Q4, the projects finally finish delivering $4 million in cash flow.

Note that by spreading the resources, not a single customer got their new product in 3 months, and all had to wait 12 months.

Now I've had the occasional skeptic scoff at this as too simplistic a view—as manufactured drama. Fair enough, let's compare it to a real-world example.

A multi-billion-dollar OEM was running over 100 programs they described as necessary. But digging a level deeper, team members only reported working on 30% of these programs in any given month. That meant two-thirds of each project's duration consisted of time spent waiting for resources.

It was just like you saw in the example. Keeping all the projects moving forward was adding wait time and overwhelming their ability to keep projects flowing rapidly. They were moving everything an inch and nothing a mile!

Instead, what if you ran the projects one after the other, as shown in Figure 4—a focused execution approach called Pipelining.

Q1	Q2	Q3	Q4
A	B	C	D

	Q1	Q2	Q3	Q4
Cash flow	$1M	$2M	$3M	$4M
Cumulative		$3M	$6M	$10M

Figure 4 – Pipelined Execution

> **"They were moving everything an inch and nothing a mile!"**

With Pipelining, Project A finishes after one quarter and begins generating revenue every quarter after that. Then Project B finishes a quarter later and so on. Since new products are like an annuity, the results keep compounding to deliver four new products and $10 million in the first year.

Compare this to starting all four early, and what do you see? Not only did you gain $6M in cash flow with the focused approach, but you also delivered 3 out of 4 projects earlier—some much earlier.

But wait, it's even worse than that. You already saw that multitasking makes work less productive. Even assuming just a 33% reduction in output, the loss of productivity due to multitasking means it will take closer to 18 months to finish the original four projects.

Compared to the six quarters of pipelined execution in Figure 5, the difference is startling. At the end of 18 months, instead of 4 products and $4 million, you have six products and $21 million in cash flow. You also have more satisfied customers.

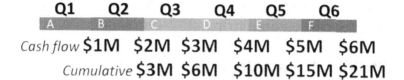

Figure 5 – Six Quarters Resourced for Full Speed

Again, let's connect this to reality. The OEM that I mentioned above found that by focusing enough resources on one project, they could work at full speed and complete a project that would have typically taken more than two years in just nine months. Those results are right in line with what you saw in the example.

The challenge is doing that on a repeatable basis without hurting other projects in your portfolio. More to come on that in the chapters that follow.

It's important not to draw the wrong conclusion from this myth. I am not saying that you should only run one project at a time. I am saying that you should only run the number of projects you can carry out at full speed. Full speed is when adding resources would not help you go any faster but removing resources would slow execution.

One final note on running too many projects simultaneously—the more crowded your pipeline becomes, the harder it is to visualize and keep track of project execution. It also tends to let lower-quality projects sneak through your governance funnel since you don't always have the time to do a thorough screening. That's a vicious circle you need to avoid.

Striking from a Solid Foundation

This has been a lengthy introduction, but there was a reason for going into such depth. The transformation to profitable *and* predictable new product growth requires striking at the roots of the problem. So it was essential to build a strong foundation of understanding from which to strike.

Remember my earlier claim—that the conventional wisdom around project and resource management is hiding 50% or more of your new product capacity? Well, I hope that the basis for that claim is now quite clear to you.

As Figure 6 illustrates, a significant portion of your capacity ends up hidden or wasted because of the myths you've just seen. That leaves you with a choice. You can continue with the status quo and simply live with your current productivity and the associated delays. You can also try to deal with it by adding more resources. But it won't be long before you are back to running too many projects and find yourself in the same situation. Neither is sustainable.

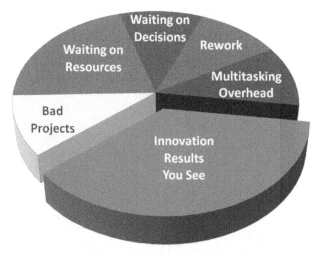

Figure 6 - Where Did All that Capacity Go?

Alternatively, in the remaining chapters, I'll share the Guided Innovation Accelerators. Strategies that strike directly at the root causes of the delays helping you drive increased innovation productivity and release hidden capacity you aren't exploiting.

As you read the strategies that follow, I encourage you to think about how they might apply to your new product innovation process–from ideation and opportunity identification to successful sales launch.

Accelerating in a New Direction

With the foundation laid so far, you're ready for a new direction—a high-performance New Product Operating System. An Innovation OS based on principles that accelerate new product growth by striking directly at the problem's roots. That is the same approach that I've been using and refining ever since that lightbulb moment when I saw how the Theory of Constraints applied to innovation.

Before Moving Forward

As you read the strategies that follow, some will challenge your thinking or offer new insights. Others will only seem like common sense. Of course, common sense and common practice aren't always the same thing. Either way, be careful about convincing your peers, colleagues, or team members that these strategies are the way to go. Nothing creates resistance, like pushing a solution you favor. The last few chapters share some strategies for building the buy-in you will need.

Additionally, I designed these accelerators to work together. Cherry-picking a few can generate a short-term bump in productivity if that's all you need. But the way to achieve significant and sustained gains is to implement them as an integrated operating system tailored to your business.

The Three Levers

Your Innovation OS has three different levers available to strike at the roots of waste—***Doing Better Projects, Doing Projects Better, and Increasing Resilience***.

Lever 1 - Doing Better Projects is about improving the quality of the opportunities that you put into your new product pipeline.

Lever 2 - Doing Projects Better is about improving your new product execution.

Lever 3 – Increasing Resilience is about the ability to weather any uncertainty that befalls your projects—to bend without breaking. Agility is the buzzword these days, but being agile is only half enough. You need to know that when your teams run into unexpected issues, that they will not only withstand the blows but will punch back.

Making these levers work sustainably requires that you drive improvement in three areas of your business—Strategy, Process, and People. Creating a high performing OS requires moving:

1. Strategy from ad hoc to Market Driven
2. Process and systems from siloed to collaborative and synchronized
3. People from busy and stressed to engaged and productive

The remaining chapters focus on the nine acceleration strategies you can use to drive change in each of these core areas.

The Guided Innovation OS Accelerators

1. Create a Firewall to Filter Out Low Impact Projects (*Strategy*)
2. Build Resilient Project Plans with Realistic Timelines (*Process*)
3. Harmonize Task and Role Definitions (*People*)
4. Control Pipeline Entry to Avoid Derailing Projects Already Underway (*Process*)
5. Synchronize Priorities for Crystal Clear Workflow (*People*)
6. Get an Early Warning—While You Can Still Recover (*Process*)
7. Huddle Daily—Even if You Think You Don't Have Time (*People*)
8. Boost your Pipeline with Better Opportunities (*Strategy*)
9. Structure for Continuous Improvement from the Start (Strategy)

Conventional project management techniques often claim to accomplish these same things. Throughout the rest of this book, I'll highlight the differences so that you can see what I mean when I say they are just hacking at the branches or applying band-aids instead of real solutions.

It's also important to recognize that a high-performance Innovation OS is not about trying to get your people to work harder. It's also not about getting them to work smarter in the same old system.

The reality is that your people want to do the right thing, but your systems and policies don't always let them. You're not happy with the results—but just imagine for a moment how frustrated they feel working in that system...

Sorry if that's too blunt. But I wouldn't be doing you any good to sugarcoat it—would I?

So you can't just train people in project management, teamwork, or problem-solving and then expect them to be able to run faster on the same old treadmill. That's a road to nowhere, and you don't want to go there. Instead, you need a systematic approach that gets you off the treadmill in the first place.

Of course, this approach isn't for everyone. Implementing these strategies requires transformation and change—at least if you want to see sustained improvement.

> **"You need a systematic approach that gets you off the treadmill..."**

Every company that's implemented these accelerators has found significant capacity hidden in plain sight. But it took a systematic approach for them to put that capacity back to work.

The strategies I'm sharing here are the same ones that our clients have implemented to create their own high productivity innovation operating systems—accelerators that have helped them get new products to market on-time and make significant and sustained gains in their innovation productivity—and all without throwing more money and people at it.

Read on, and you'll see how these strategies strike directly at the root causes behind the myths covered earlier. Then decide for yourself if they make sense for your business.

A Word About Project Budgets

Throughout the rest of this book, you may notice that I don't address project budgets. There's a reason for that. No question, most new product projects over-run their budgets. So the tools that I use do allow for budget tracking. But I've simply found that if you strike at the roots of the delays, exceeding your project budget is rarely a problem.

That's because the drivers in budget overruns are:
- Missed handoffs
- Confusion about requirements
- Scope creep
- Rework for prototypes, molds, tooling, etc.
- Expediting and change fees

That last one, expediting and change fees, is a hidden budget hit that can easily bypass your financial controls.

Moreover, in new products, the bulk of the budget is usually staffing. Regardless of the games companies play to allocate costs, staffing is a fixed expense, not an out-of-pocket one. It's different if you are building a skyscraper or even just a house. In that case, materials are a much larger part, and contractor labor is variable.

Get your execution and timeline under control, and budget performance will fall into line.

Accelerator #1: Create a Firewall to Filter Out Low Impact Projects

A Lever 1 Strategy—focused on **Doing Better Projects**—ensuring the quality of the opportunities you put into your execution pipeline

If pressed to explain the value of governance in one sentence, I would cite the late Peter Drucker, who said, "There is nothing more useless than to do efficiently that which should not have been done in the first place."

A powerful statement, to be sure—but let's go just a few levels deeper and share some of the elements behind it.

The Feasibility Firewall

"We don't know how to say no." It's a common complaint inside companies, and the results can be profound. Without effective governance serving as a firewall for your innovation pipeline, it's easy for low impact, low feasibility, or poorly defined opportunities to clog the system and sap your resources.

> **"There is nothing more useless than doing efficiently that which should not be done at all."**

To further illustrate this, as shown in Figure 7, a long term study of firms in the electronics industry by Ogawa and Ketner [4] showed that the top 20% of companies canceled only 1% of the projects they had started—meaning they wasted only a small amount of R&D or engineering resources.

In contrast, the remaining 80% of companies canceled nearly 20% of their projects—meaning that they wasted almost 20 times as many R&D and engineering resources.

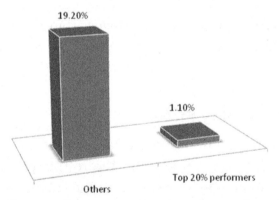

19.20%

1.10%

Top 20% performers

Others

Top performers cancel underperforming projects early – before they use resources

Figure 7 – Projects Canceled After Using R&D/Engineering Resources

Before you conclude that the top 20% were just development rockstars, you should know that both groups canceled the same percentage of projects overall. The difference is that the rockstars canceled projects early in the process before they could waste too many resources.

The study also showed that the companies in the top 20% delivered new products to market in half the time of their competitors and achieved nearly double the percentage of new product profits.

At its core, that's what governance is all about—making sure that you only use your constrained resources on the best projects. The conventional wisdom encourages us to "Just Do It." But ask yourself if every project your company is working on deserves the resources it is getting.

Just think about the projects your firm has run that never finished or didn't deliver the sales bump promised. And when these projects start to struggle, resource consumption spikes, delaying other higher probability opportunities.

The result is that the top 20% of what you work on delivers 80% of the impact. So do you really need to work on the bottom 80%? Not if you have a resilient governance process that pushes those underperformers to the bottom of the list and allows better, more deserving opportunities to rise to the top.

The first step in establishing this type of governance is to screen every new product idea or opportunity—first against your own new product strategy and then against what I call the "**Big 5**" feasibilities:

1. **Commercial** – Can this product alleviate a significant limitation for the customer, and is there a strong likelihood that the customer's financial payback will be attractive enough to entice purchase? Even if the answer is yes, can you easily reach and convince the buyers with this problem?

2. **Technical** – Do you have a technology solution available, or does it have to be developed, and what is the level of uncertainty? Is a proof of concept or prototype warranted?

3. **Manufacturing** – What are the supply chain implications involved, and what kind of investment might be required?

4. **Regulatory** – Are there any government agencies that must approve before you can produce or sell your new product, and what is the timing required for approval?

5. **Intellectual Property** – You may want to patent your technology, but here we're looking at it from the other direction. Do you have the freedom to operate without violating others' patents?

After answering these questions, you can determine if the investment you would have to make and the return you could get justify moving forward with development.

Wondering about the order chosen for the different feasibilities? Commercial is listed first because product managers can often evaluate it with minimal effort from your technical resources. And if you don't understand the customer and product economics—let's just agree that your next step should not be development work!

The Prioritized Backlog

Just because a project makes it through your feasibility firewall doesn't mean you should start it immediately—or even at all. If this sounds contradictory, imagine that six good projects come through governance simultaneously, but you only have enough resources to handle three of them. As you saw in the introduction, starting all six would mean that all of them would take two to three times as long.

Instead, the next step in governance is forced-ranking the projects you have. Then you place them on a prioritized backlog waiting for resources. I'll cover how to schedule the move off the backlog and into execution in a later strategy on controlling pipeline entry.

The best way to rank projects is using return per hour for your most constrained resource. In this case, the return is the cash flow from sales less any out-of-pocket investments such as tooling or prototyping services. Without going into the mathematical proof, if software engineering is your most loaded and hardest to add resource, you maximize throughput for your portfolio by prioritizing based on return per software engineering hour. However, even using return per total development hour would likely improve your results.

Full-Kit Review

Full-Kitting is an element of the Critical Chain Project Management (CCPM) solution that you'll hear more about in the next chapter. But the idea behind full-kitting is that you shouldn't start a project without having everything you need to finish—the so-called full-kit.

For example, a painter shouldn't start a job without first having all the tools and materials such as paint, masking tape, drop cloths, brushes, rollers, ladder, screwdrivers, etc. And most importantly, they shouldn't start until the client has picked the paint color.

Similarly, for new product innovation, every opportunity needs a Full-Kit Review before the project starts. This review ensures that the cross-functional project team has all the information they need regarding requirements and specifications and an appropriate plan to deliver the new product. It also resolves questions or inconsistencies before the project starts.

When full-kitting is complete, you should have all the elements for a project charter. Essentially an agreement by all stakeholders specifying what you will be developing. In its simplest form, it looks something like "Complete the sales launch for product X by Y date. Required features are A, B & C as outlined in Document D."

The charter may also have timing requirements for deliverables—more on that later. And it may specify who owns the charter and must approve any changes. But only make it as complicated as is absolutely necessary to deliver the expected results.

In some projects, you might find it challenging to lock down features and requirements early on. Situations like this require mini-learning cycles. Consider structuring the project with customer-facing exploration and technical proof of concept tasks during the first several cycles where requirements and tradeoffs have room to emerge. More about this later in Accelerator #8 – Boost Your Pipeline with Better Opportunities. The earlier, the better, but this work is required well before design freeze. It's also essential that the project team and leadership come together after each cycle to understand the tradeoffs and assumptions.

Cost of A Days Delay

At this stage, the team should also identify and calculate the cost of a day's delay—a handy bit of information for both force ranking and execution.

If the team working on the project knows the cost of a day's delay—often in the tens of thousands of dollars and sometimes even into the millions—they can make much better decisions throughout the project.

A healthcare products company was struggling with a project that had gone on for far too long. They were trying to create the perfect design. Meanwhile, their competitor's less-than-perfect new product was continuing to eat away at their position and take market share.

After this had gone on for months, the general manager finally threw his hands up in desperation and told the team, "Not having this product on the market is costing us 50 thousand dollars in lost profits each and every day!"

When faced with the fact that three months of trying to perfect the design had cost the company nearly half a million dollars, the engineering manager was stunned. Had she known what the delay was costing, she would have launched a "good-enough" version months earlier.

Benefits of Effective Governance

Governance pays significant benefits by killing questionable projects before they can waste resources and delay other programs. A client was planning an extension of their high-efficiency industrial line into the commercial market. But with the governance that we established, they realized that they had not done sufficient payback analysis to understand the pricing required to get customers to switch. After learning that the selling price needed to be lower than even the best case expected manufacturing cost, they killed the project. That saved hundreds of thousands of dollars and redirected those resources to better opportunities.

Potential Pitfalls

Building a governance mechanism and ranking system that is both effective and responsive takes careful consideration. Here are a few pitfalls you'll want to avoid.

Pitfall #1 Bureaucratic Governance – It's a tricky balance to add governance and at the same time remain agile. But with careful planning and communication, it is possible.

You need a standard governance approach, but you don't want to make the mistake of trying to force-fit the same evaluation across different classes of new products. What works best in R&D or NPD is quite different from what fits in an OEM component or engineer-to-order environment.

Pitfall #2 Pretend Governance – Good governance has integrity, is transparent, and is well communicated so that people continue to believe in and work within the system. Suppose you turn a blind eye to certain people who breeze through or even skip governance. In that case, you run the risk of letting it become a political process that is easily ignored—or even worse, avoided.

Another example of pretend governance is when low-margin opportunities for specific customers are deemed strategic and spared scrutiny. Allow this to go on too often, and the organization will lose respect for the entire process.

That's not to say there aren't times when you have to take on lower margin opportunities for strategic reasons. But with the right approach, you can sometimes turn these low margin opportunities around—not by saying, "No," but instead saying, " Not Now " or "Not at that price."

Pitfall #3 Static Governance – Good governance is also dynamic. If you have three projects on the backlog and an even better one comes along, do you have the flexibility to reprioritize?

Situations like this can be a real challenge in an environment involving customer-driven work with already agreed due dates.

Should a large project from a small, non-strategic customer ever move ahead of a small project from a strategic customer? Should a small project for your largest customer push a big project from a small non-strategic customer to the back of the line? There are no set answers to these questions, and managing a dynamic backlog requires full engagement and transparency from your management team.

Pitfall #4 Thinking You Are Different – Sometimes, I run into managers who claim their projects are "pretty straightforward" and feasibility or full kitting review doesn't really apply to their programs.

One example of this happened when working with a large OEM parts manufacturer. They had a well-established pricing model and felt that it should be obvious which projects were feasible. After rolling out their new operating system, they were surprised to see how many new opportunities required re-scoping with customers after feasibility and full-kit review.

After adding this full-kit step, they found very few projects getting hung up in the later stages. As a result, customer complaints about new product delays dropped from several per week to one or two per year—and that's with hundreds of projects every year.

Pitfall #5 Confusing Technology Development with Product Development – Try to avoid including technology development in product development projects. The uncertainty and number of learning loops make these fundamentally different kinds of projects. Trying to do technology development as part of a new product project almost guarantees delays.

Instead, think about technology development projects as separate work you need to do to keep your product development toolbox full. That implies you should choose the technology development projects you work on based on your insights into unmet needs and technology gaps in your focus market segments.

What's Next?

This chapter has summarized the governance elements required for your high-performance Innovation OS—a disciplined system for giving only the best opportunities access to new product development resources. In the next chapter, I'll cover strategies for building robust projects and realistic timelines that both your team and your customers will understand and accept.

Accelerator #2: Build Resilient Project Plans with Realistic Timelines

A Lever 2 & 3 Strategy—focused on *Doing Projects Better* and *Increasing Resilience*

Once you've decided that a new product opportunity is consistent with your strategy, is feasible, and meets your financial hurdles, the next step is to create a robust plan and realistic timeline that your team and customers can understand and accept.

I've advised many companies struggling with new product issues, and they've all had one thing in common. None ever started with a coherent approach to project planning in place. That's not to say good planning is sufficient. But it is necessary.

Companies without good planning fall into one of two camps. Half will admit they don't do any real project planning. The other half claim to do serious project planning—but what they do is a far cry from it.

One multi-billion-dollar OEM manufacturer struggling with new products is a case in point. Their projects were typically lasting 2-3 years, but the project plans they showed me only had 20-30 tasks. Not an unusual situation.

To anyone that's ever run this scale of project, 20-30 tasks for a multi-year project doesn't pass the smell test. So I asked them if these were the only tasks in the project—which, of course, they weren't. After some hemming and hawing, they admitted these "tasks" were only major milestones that might last 3-9 months with tens if not hundreds of sub-tasks missing from the plan.

Project managers rarely looked at these so-called plans. Instead, they were running projects with task lists kept in Excel spreadsheets or One Note documents—think about that for a moment.

These were major, multi-year projects with millions of dollars in investment. Moreover, the revenue at stake for every day of delay dwarfed the investment—especially if they missed a model year launch. But they were running these projects with ad hoc lists hidden away in spreadsheets and note sharing tools.

It's also helpful to examine how project managers created those lists. Most did so based on their personal experience and understanding of what was required. Of course, there's never time to pull together a cross-functional team to build a plan. So they were rarely taking advantage of the tremendous tribal knowledge available across the organization—the dozens of designers, engineers, purchasing professionals, testing, and quality experts with deep insights into the work and its challenges.

Is it any wonder they were frustrated with delays? Not exactly an ideal approach to building the kind of engagement and commitment you are expecting from your new product teams.

Lists Are Not Plans

When lists substitute for project plans, you can't visualize what needs to happen next. Picture this for a moment. Your team is sitting down to discuss the project status and what needs to happen next. They have a list of all the remaining tasks in front of them. How easily can they visualize which task the team should work on next? And are there others another team member could do at the same time?

The problem is that lists are linear—not showing the real relationships between tasks. You do Task A, then B, then C, and so on. "To Do" lists like this can work for an individual since, as the earlier multitasking exercise proved, you can only do one cognitive activity at a time. But that's not the case for a project team.

In contrast, the complexity of new product development requires that many different workstreams proceed simultaneously. These consist of mechanical, electrical, and even software tasks. They also include functional tasks such as procurement or manufacturing. Additionally, integration tasks bring these workstreams together many times throughout a project. But how can anyone manage that type of complexity using a one-dimensional list?

The alternative that I'm suggesting doesn't have to be complicated. Before any program enters the execution pipeline, just assemble a cross-functional team to follow these simple steps—what I call Guided Innovation Planning:

1. Plan for Obstacles
2. Build the Project Network
3. Add Resources & Durations
4. Identify the Critical Chain
5. Crunch the Plan

1. Plan for Obstacles [5]

How many times have you seen projects derailed by obstacles that the team should have anticipated? It's easy to miss these issues because everyone is so busy and moving so fast that they don't stop to ask the obvious questions.

With the clear and unambiguous project charter developed in full-kitting, every project leader needs to ask this counterintuitive question at the start of planning—especially when working in a new area. "What are all the possible reasons you could dream of that would cause this project to fail?"

You can view this as a sort of risk identification and mitigation exercise. But it's more than that. Not only does Guided Innovation Planning help identify the obstacles that your plan must overcome, but it also helps build commitment and engagement. No sitting on your hands in the planning session and then playing that passive-aggressive game of saying, "If only you had asked me..."

> **"What are all the possible reasons you could dream of that would cause this project to fail?"**

2. Build the Project Network

Once you've identified the potential obstacles, how do you get around them? Instead of a task list, your cross-functional project team needs to build a project network that shows the relationships between tasks.

With Guided Innovation Planning, the team starts by planning in reverse. Beginning with the final deliverable and then using Post-its on a large whiteboard or wall, they work back task-by-task through all of the identified obstacles—one Post-it per task. With each, they ask, "And what needs to happen before this task can start?" or, "What do we need to do to get around this obstacle so this task can be successful?"

As shown in Figure 8, the result is a clear and powerful picture of the work to be done.

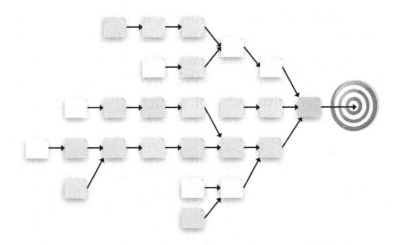

Figure 8 - Guided Innovation Planning Roadmap

While it requires an investment of time upfront to build good project networks, that investment pays big dividends in execution. That's where work flows like a relay race, obstacles clear early, and individuals work with limited multitasking and interruptions.

Many companies find that once they have built a handful of these networks, certain elements are repeatable. That means they can create project templates that significantly speed the planning for each new project. A team simply starts with a template, configures what it can, and modifies the rest accordingly by adding or deleting tasks as required. I've seen teams get project planning down to a few hours or less with this approach—well worth the investment.

A note on extremely large, complex projects—You may also decide that a project is so large or geographically complex that you want to manage it as a group of smaller subprojects all connected back to a master project. The approach is the same as above, with each subproject getting its own network.

3. Determine Task Durations

Here's where things really begin to diverge from conventional project planning approaches. The key to creating robust and resilient plans lies in a different method called Critical Chain Project Management. [6] CCPM is a fundamentally different approach to project management rooted in the Theory of Constraints. It has enabled thousands of companies to exceed 90% on-time performance for their projects.

As you saw in the introduction, traditional project management pads the project with safety in each of the tasks by using high probability estimates with a 90-95% chance of finishing on time. No one wants to admit it, but that means many project timelines are 2-3 times longer than the actual "touch-time" to account for waiting, interruptions, and inevitable problems.

As you also saw in the introduction, student syndrome and other procrastination behaviors waste that safety putting your project due date at risk when any unexpected issues arise.

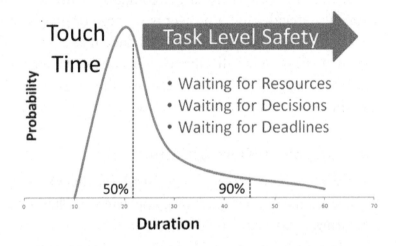

Figure 9 - Probability of Task Completion

CCPM differs from conventional methods because it takes that safety out of individual tasks and instead uses aggressive estimates with only a 50% chance of finishing on time—so-called touch-time estimates. As shown in Figure 9, a rule-of-thumb is that touch times should be half the length of 90% probability estimates.

You then put half of the time removed from the critical chain tasks back as a shared buffer at the end of the project. Why only half? Because with a 50% chance of finishing on time combined with relay racer execution, some early and late finishes will cancel each other. As shown in Figure 10, the project timeline combines the critical chain and the project buffer.

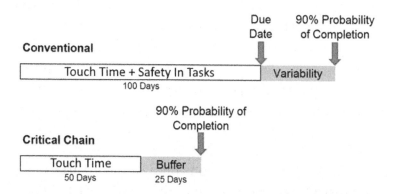

Figure 10 - CCPM vs. Conventional Timelines

A project traditionally planned at 100 days has 50 days of safety buried in the tasks. Instead, a Critical Chain plan has 50 days of work duration (the critical chain) followed by 25 days of project buffer for an overall length of 75 days—a 25% reduction. But the CCPM project also has a much higher likelihood of finishing on-time. That's because the buffer protects the due date instead of encouraging procrastination.

So CCPM project plans appear to be 25% shorter. However, with the higher likelihood of finishing on time, the effective reduction in project length is far larger than 25%.

4. Identify the Critical Chain

As you saw above, there are two primary components to the timeline—the critical chain and the project buffer. The critical chain is your project's constraint—the longest sequence of tasks without any planned multi-tasking. The distinction is vital since traditional critical-path methods encourage you to bake multi-tasking into your plans giving you an unrealistic timeline.

For example, let's say your plan calls for three tasks for fabricating prototype circuit boards, each taking one day in the fabrication area. These are independent tasks, and traditional critical path planning would schedule them for the same day. However, you only have one circuit board fabrication cell, so that is not possible.

Baking this into the plan at one day would have underestimated the timeline by two days. Any competent CCPM software can look at resources to prevent this from happening—more about software at the end of this chapter.

The rule of thumb used in Figure 10 is that the buffer added at the end of the project should be half the critical chain's length. Again, that's not really something you have to worry about either. Most CCPM software can automatically determine the critical chain and add the necessary buffers to protect the timeline.

In the software-generated timeline shown in Figure 11, the darker solid bars represent the critical chain tasks. The lighter bars represent feeding chain tasks—tasks that aren't on the critical chain but feed into it at different points in the project.

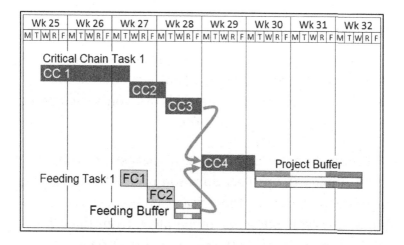

Figure 11 – Critical Chain Timeline

The length of each task shown reflects touch-time, and the software adds a time buffer equal to 50% of the CC duration at the end of the project. That's the three-zone bar shown at the end of the critical chain. The buffer is there to act as a shock absorber protecting the timeline. During execution, the zones fill in as your project consumes buffer.

A word of warning on interpreting the CC Timeline—Tasks will not finish on the dates shown, and the project is not likely to finish on the date shown for the last task. So you shouldn't expect to finish before 80% of the buffer has been consumed. At least not with any regularity. It's something executives and managers must get used to-not too hard after they've experienced how well it works.

5. Crunch the Plan

Since the critical chain is your project's constraint, it is also your leverage point. Another valuable benefit then is that the critical chain shows you which tasks control your project's duration.

Feeding chain tasks are still necessary, but they don't impact the project duration unless they begin to overrun projects on the critical chain. On the other hand, any time added or taken away from the critical chain directly impacts the project's duration.

That means that the only way to crunch or shorten the project duration is to scrub the critical chain looking for tasks that could run in parallel without multitasking.

Figure 12 shows the timeline in Figure 11 after crunching it to deliver six days earlier (four days of task time and two days of buffer). This new timeline assumes CC2 can start when CC1 is halfway complete.

Your planning team must be judicious here, though. Changes like this can add significant financial or technical risk. While it might be worth it, you need to have clear guidelines. What risks is the team allowed to take and which require management involvement?

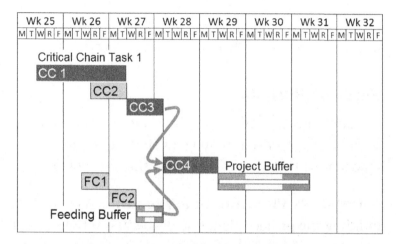

Figure 12 - Crunched Timeline

Your planning teams should also be encouraged to look for unnecessary steps in the plan or the process, especially if you start with a template. While well-meaning, most gated processes try to treat every project the same. There may be some that don't apply to every project. So you need to be able to zero them out when appropriate.

Benefits of Robust Project Planning

A component manufacturer identified that the wait time for parts and tooling was almost always on their projects' critical chain. Not only that, these tasks comprised more than half of the critical chain—meaning that they were essentially determining the lead time for most projects.

By focusing efforts on these procurement activities, they were able to identify ways to shorten them and significantly reduce the lead time for new products.

Potential Pitfalls

Planning is a critical discipline, and there are several pitfalls your project managers and cross-functional teams must be aware of when creating their plans.

Pitfall #1 Planning in a Vacuum - As you start building the project plan, one of the first pitfalls you'll want to avoid is a lack of cross-functional involvement. People are busy, so it can be hard to gain their participation in planning. But it's essential if you want realistic timelines and your team's commitment. Planning carried out by project managers in a vacuum just won't get you there.

Pitfall #2 Buffer Deniers – Inevitably, there's a manager, often on the commercial side where time pressure is highest, who will campaign to eliminate the buffer—claiming that projects now take longer. You need to be able to show that this isn't true. Project plans will be shorter by at least 25%, and actual durations will be as much as 50% shorter since traditional projects are often late.

It is unlikely your project will finish without using a significant portion of its buffer. Only a few percent at best. So working without a project buffer is like walking a high wire without a safety net in a windstorm. No matter your agility, you are almost guaranteeing a disastrous finish. Plus, if you mess with the project buffer, the organization will start sneaking it back as safety in the individual tasks, anyway. In no time at all, you'll be back where you started—not exactly the kind of predictability you want to build your business on.

Additionally, in upcoming chapters, you will see how the buffer becomes a critical tool for measuring and managing the risk of missing the due date. A capability at the core of effective execution.

Pitfall #3 Sizing Tasks to Meet the Due Date – Some companies create detailed plans with professional-looking Gantt charts, but then size the tasks not to reflect reality but to give the appearance the project can meet the deadline.

Working with an electronics company that had this problem, I heard a planning discussion where the conversation regularly went something like this:

Project Manager: "How long will it take you to finish that task?"

Team Member: "When do you need it?"

If I hadn't intervened, the project manager would have published a timeline that met the desired deadline, but it would have had no chance of finishing on time. And an organization that agrees to unrealistic timelines doesn't end up with high commitment and engagement levels. Nor do they please customers.

Pitfall #4 No Peer Review – Cross-functional planning helps identify each workstream's essential tasks and how they integrate. But even then, the folks involved in the planning may be too close to see the problems for themselves. After completing plans for your larger projects, it is always helpful to have a so-called non-advocate peer review. This step is where a subject matter expert, with no interest in the outcome, critiques the plan. Fresh eyes like this help guard against groupthink in your projects.

Pitfall #5 Micro or Macro-Managing Tasks – It takes practice to correctly do this type of work breakdown. A common mistake is to size tasks either too large or too small. Too large, and you won't be able to visualize flow effectively. Too small, and you'll burden the organization with unnecessary details and what will look like too many hand-offs. An ideal task size is somewhere between one and three days—the exception being long waiting tasks.

Pitfall #6 Waiting Tasks – Tasks with an extended waiting component, such as extended testing or procurement of tooling or long-lead-time parts, can make it challenging to visualize progress and resource loading. So try to structure tasks and model resources with this distinction in mind to see where resources are needed more clearly.

As mentioned earlier, these long waiting tasks have an outsized impact on the critical chain. Also, the rule-of-thumb that the 90% probability duration is twice the touch time doesn't apply in most waiting tasks. Since most CCPM software adds a buffer automatically, you must find a workable and repeatable way to estimate these tasks.

A starting point is to size these tasks at 70% of the promised or expected lead time if there is little variability expected as with a highly reliable supplier or a fixed duration test with a high likelihood of passing. Alternatively, if there is significant doubt about the duration or the possibility of success, use the full estimate. In both cases, the system should still add a project buffer.

A Note on CCPM Software

People regularly ask if it's necessary to use Critical Chain software like Exepron, Pro-Chain, or Concerto. With the cloud-based tools now available, I wouldn't recommend trying to operate without them.

There are CCPM add-ins available for MS Project, but they aren't easy to use, nor are they well-suited to multi-project environments. Additionally, they require project managers with MS Project expertise, which is getting harder to find.

Alternatively, cloud-based Critical Chain systems automate all but the network building and individual progress reporting. That includes project staggering, project status reporting, and many of the analysis and reporting tools that the team needs to stay on track, as described in the following chapters.

You can learn more about the CCPM software my clients use at:

GuidedInnovation.com/Software-Choices

What's Next?

This chapter has summarized how a high-performance Innovation OS can ensure that every project starts with a robust and realistic plan. In the next chapter, I'll explain the part that task and role definition plays in keeping people engaged.

Accelerator #3: Harmonize Task and Role Definitions

A Lever 2 & 3 Strategy—focused on *Doing Projects Better* and *Increasing Resilience*

This accelerator may seem like it is only a refinement of the previous one, Building Resilient Plans. But it's still worth a short chapter because the way you build your plans has a significant influence on the people side of innovation productivity. Intangibles like motivation and engagement are essential to resilient execution.

In Engines of Disharmony, [7] Eli Goldratt detailed the conflicts between people that sap motivation, commitment, and engagement. Those engines are:

1. Not understanding how you or others should be contributing to the company's success

2. Conflicts about the work to be done

3. Work or work rules that are no longer necessary but still exist due to inertia

4. Gaps between responsibility and authority

The way that you define project tasks and assign responsibilities can eliminate many of these issues.

Clarifying Contribution & Responsibilities

You would think that in a project-based environment, like new products, everyone would understand what they and their colleagues are supposed to do. And the same is true as far as responsibility and authority. But that's one of the things missing in many companies—especially when new product plans are simply ad hoc checklists. They lack the necessary clarity as to which department is responsible for which tasks, who is assigned to do the work, and even who must ultimately sign off.

You might also think that who does what should be obvious. But when helping clients build project networks, I continue to be surprised by the lack of clarity around which department is responsible for specific tasks. Some are obvious, but others end up provoking heated arguments. This lack of clarity invites confusion and finger-pointing during execution—not a great way to drive engagement. So it's critical to go through the network task by task and reach agreement on which group is responsible. It's also helpful to do so in a way that you can repurpose as part of future project templates.

Clarifying Work to Be Done

Another area that can create friction is task definition or task exit criteria. Imagine what happens when a team member hands off a finished task to the next task manager, and later they discover that some part of the previous task was left unfinished. Maybe it was something simple like entering information into a bill of material, or perhaps it was something more complicated like a design calculation. In either case, it slows things down and creates disharmony when the next task manager has to stop and chase down the information. In more complex situations, it can also create costly rework.

To prevent this friction, create a standard set of definitions for every task in your project templates– Definitions of Done. For example, *Update Manufacturing Plan* is the kind of activity that seems simple enough but where misalignment is likely. It can mean different things to different people, different departments, and different companies. Here's an example of the level of detail that you need. It is also essential to solicit cross-functional input on these definitions.

The purpose of this task is to update the manufacturing plan before the Stage 5 gate review. This task should not be marked complete until you have:

- *Created process map of proposed manufacturing process*

- *Developed plan for tooling, routing, programming, and fixturing*
- *Completed Design for Manufacturing (DFM) and Assembly (DFA) checklist*
- *Published Lessons Learned Report for the mock-up production run*
- *Completed Risk Assessment for costs, quality, lead times, and follow-on capacity issues*
- *Integrated Quality Plan into the Mfg Plan*

Eliminating Unnecessary Tasks

It may seem obvious that as systems and processes change, you should update the tasks in your project templates to reflect that. But inertia can be difficult to overcome. So your process owner should conduct regular reviews as part of continuous improvement efforts. They must ensure that the work reflects the current reality as systems and processes are improved and updated.

Potential Pitfalls

Task and role definition goes a long way towards eliminating roadblocks to engagement, but there are several pitfalls you need to avoid.

Pitfall #1 Inflexibility in Execution– There's a dichotomy that you need to be aware of here. Every task should have an owner or task manager, but that doesn't mean that only the assigned task manager can execute the task. When a project begins using too much buffer, one way to recover is to flex resources; especially when the assigned task manager is busy with another task. When this happens, don't let overly-rigid task assignments hold you back if someone else can do the work.

Pitfall #2 Gaps in Preparation and Approval – A typical product development project can have dozens of sign-offs embedded within project tasks. The project manager may be responsible for preparing the gate review package. But they do not have the ultimate authority to approve the next phase of the project, which falls upon the management team. For that reason, it's helpful to break work like this into separate preparation and approval tasks.

What's Next?

This chapter has outlined how your Innovation OS can increase engagement and reduce the friction that causes disharmony through unclear role and task definition. In the next chapter, I'll explain how to manage the release of your well-planned projects to execution in a way that maximizes throughput and avoids derailing the projects already underway.

Accelerator #4: Control Pipeline Entry to Maximize Speed and Resilience

A Lever 2 & 3 Strategy—focused on *Doing Projects Better* and *Increasing Resilience*

In the previous chapter, you learned how to build harmony with clear task definitions and responsibilities—critical to keeping people engaged and committed. You might also have noticed that the planning process considers each project in isolation from the others. It just isn't practical to do otherwise. But they still must be executed in the real world. A world where multiple projects compete for limited shared resources. This chapter provides a strategy for dealing with that disconnect, crucial for increasing both speed and resilience.

Every product development organization has a limited or constrained bandwidth—the number of projects it can run at full speed. And as you've seen already, letting in more projects than you have the bandwidth to run means that each of your projects will spend time unnecessarily waiting for resources. And that makes every project take longer.

Like the example in Myth #3, I lead a workshop exercise using a simulated product development company with a bandwidth of four projects—each lasting six months when resourced at full speed.

If the company respects that bandwidth, they finish two projects per quarter, maintain a cycle time (project duration) of six months, and deliver predictable growth in new product cashflow.

However, if they allow just one extra project into execution each quarter, the results are markedly different. With too many projects sharing constrained resources, cycle time climbs to 22 months, and cashflow drops by about 66% over two years.

It's a real eye-opener for the executives in this workshop to see the effect on cycle time and revenue. After all, it's only one extra project per quarter. How bad could that be? The problem is that once you get buried underneath too many projects, it's hard to get out again.

I usually encounter a few skeptics when teaching this, but it's only simple math. Once you reach your bandwidth, every extra project you add makes the others take longer and delays cash flow and its compound effects.

Of course, the simulation would be useless if it didn't match what happens in the real world. I've seen these same kinds of numbers play out in companies across industries. It's not unusual to compress projects taking 2-3 years down to a year or less.

Respecting Your Process Constraint

Now at this point, conventional wisdom would mistakenly tell you, "Okay, if we can't overload our pipeline anymore, let's at least make sure we keep everyone busy."

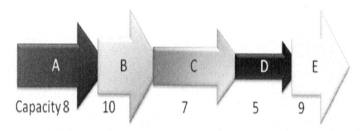

Figure 13 – Constrained Process

Figure 13 is a simple example to illustrate the point. Think of innovation as a process where work flows from Function A to B and so on. If Step D's capacity is constrained to 5 units/period, does it help to keep Step B busy at 10 units/period? Of course not, because busy is not the same as productive. It only creates excess work in process (WIP) and increases cycle time as samples piles up in front of Steps C and D, further eroding throughput.

Limiting Capacity Utilization for Maximum Throughput

Once you have identified your constraint, conventional wisdom would again tell you to operate the constraint at the highest utilization possible.

Can you guess what my response is going to be? That's right. Conventional wisdom would again lead you down the wrong path.

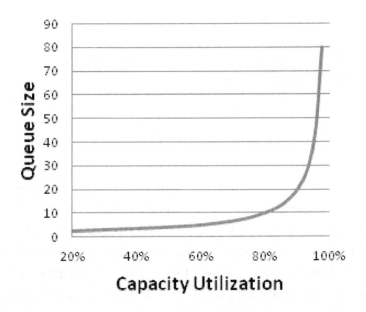

Figure 14 – Impact of Capacity on Cycle Time

Figure 14 shows how queue size or waiting time increases exponentially with capacity utilization. [8] The impact is relatively mild until you near 70-80%.

Beyond that, waiting time becomes unstable and highly vulnerable to variation. So operating any resource near full capacity creates instability that reduces both throughput and predictability.

The best way to picture this is to imagine driving home from the office on a downtown freeway late in the evening. If a road crew has one lane shut down doing repairs, how much will that add to your travel time? A minute or two at most—the variance will hardly be noticeable in your overall travel time.

Now, how much more would it add to your travel time if that same roadwork still has a lane shutdown when you return to your office the next morning during rush hour? There's a pretty good chance you won't make your 8:00 AM staff meeting—the variance is now a much more noticeable percentage of your trip time.

That's why busy cities use the onramp metering you see during rush hour on major freeways. If you've never experienced one, they force drivers to queue up and then dribble them into the busy highway one car at a time.

The primary reason for metering is not to limit the number of vehicles on the roadway since traffic is already in the zone of unstable utilization. Instead, it smooths out the flow to prevent the interruptions caused when cars enter in large slugs rather than in a steady drip.

Project Scheduling

Is allowing too many programs into execution at the same time jamming up your pipeline? It's only common sense that the more projects underway, the longer everything takes to reach the market. Now you can also see that it also makes product development flow more chaotic and less predictable. That's just the opposite of the resilience you need.

But with conventional approaches, you see this impact ignored repeatedly. Without a mechanism to control and release new projects based on bandwidth or resource availability, it's easy to let in too many new projects without finishing or pruning the old ones. Eventually, you reach a point where the flow slows down, and it's hard to see any real progress. That's what I call glacial innovation.

So how can you address this systematically in new product development? Well, you want to take advantage of both effects—utilization control and metering. You need a system that tracks the expected workload for your current work and allows you to evaluate the impact of incoming programs. The solution is to monitor the capacity utilization and then limit new project entry to keep your loading in a target range below 80%.

You start by creating a prioritized backlog list—the same backlog mentioned in Accelerator #1 – Create a

Firewall to Filter Out Low Impact Projects. These are the governance-approved projects that you haven't started yet. Whenever you want to add a new project to that backlog, you evaluate its impact on the portfolio and schedule a start date that doesn't interfere with the flow of projects already running—in effect, metering traffic into your execution pipeline.

A simple way to create that type of pull system is with a virtual drum. Let's say that your pilot plant is your constraint and that it can run five projects at the same time. In that case, you would set a work-in-process (WIP) limit of four projects in the pilot plant. Then you would only pull a new project into the overall pipeline when the pilot plant finished a task dropping its WIP below four projects.

Why four and not five? Because you don't want to exceed 80% of capacity and stray into that unstable zone.

Unfortunately, the virtual drum has two drawbacks. First, bandwidth can be very fluid and difficult to measure—especially if your projects differ significantly in size or have wide swings in resource utilization within a project. An example would be zero-resource tasks such as waiting for long lead time parts and tooling, external certification labs, or even customer approvals. Additionally, the virtual drum can be hard to sustain with people continually pushing for a higher WIP limit to accommodate their projects.

A better approach is a dynamic one where your project planning and execution software does the work of monitoring your bandwidth and its projected utilization. After all, you've already included resources in your project plans, so why not take advantage of that information to manage capacity. Every new project entering the portfolio goes through a scheduling exercise to find a start date that does not risk derailing the projects already underway.

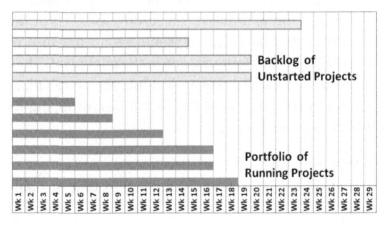

Figure 15 - Backlog Projects Waiting Scheduling by Week

To show you how that would work, let's say that you have a portfolio of already running projects represented in Figure 15 by the darker horizontal bars. The top half's lighter bars are your backlog—all the projects you have already created plans for and now need to schedule. The right end of each bar indicates the expected finish date. The length of the bars represents the expected duration of each project.

The weekly resource loading chart in Figure 16 shows what would happen if you let all the projects into execution at once. The workload would overwhelm Resources A, B, and C, making it impossible to complete any of the projects in the time planned. You would also be encouraging multitasking and its adverse effects.

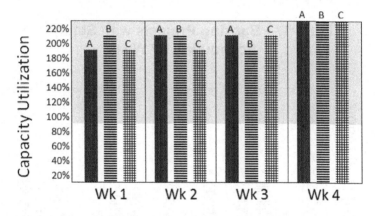

Figure 16 - Weekly Resource Capacity Loading

The solution is to schedule the projects into the portfolio with a stagger between the start dates. No worries—this is also something that your project planning software should do automatically or at least simplify.

Figure 17 shows the scheduled projects as lighter bars with the left edges (start dates) pushed or staggered to the right (later in time) to prevent resource overloading.

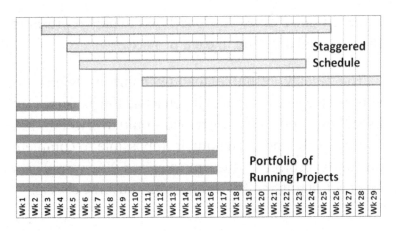

Figure 17 - Backlog Projects with Staggered Scheduling by Week

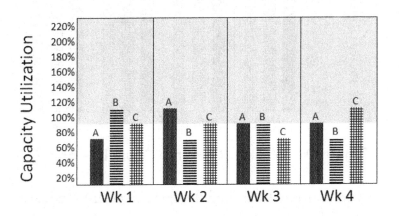

Figure 18 - Loading after Staggered Scheduling

The result in Figure 18 shows how the staggering reduced resource utilization for all three below 80% across the planning horizon.

With this approach, you can also reverse engineer a picture of your actual resource needs. Simply set the start date for each project to deliver the required due date and then adjust resource levels until you bring loading near 80%. You now have a picture of how many of each resource type you need. As long as you model your resources appropriately, this approach works as well for full-time positions as it does for flexible resources such as outsourcing firms, contractors, and temps.

Benefits of Regulating Pipeline Entry

Respecting bandwidth and managing your pipeline in this manner strikes directly at the roots of the chaos that so often distracts new product organizations. It allows you to reach a level of predictability you may have doubted possible after years of experience with conventional approaches.

As mentioned in the introduction, a company using this approach in the industrial steam generation equipment market saw significant gains. Their projects had slowed to a crawl, but after beginning to control the number of active projects, they were able to cut time-to-market by more than half.

Potential Pitfalls

Scheduling projects into your pipeline at a rate that doesn't derail projects already underway is critical to resilient execution. Here are a few pitfalls you will want to avoid.

Pitfall #1 Not Taking Bandwidth Seriously - This is one of the most critical steps in the process—where your projects meet the reality of shared resources in a multi-project environment. It's also where they can quickly become derailed.

Without a considered approach to modeling and measuring resource utilization, people will continue to challenge the data and try to ignore the recommendations so their projects can start sooner.

Pitfall #2 Fear of Saying No or Not Now – What good is it to have visibility into resource loading and then ignore it? But some managers don't like the idea of a backlog. They see it as a sign of weakness vs. the sign of discipline and predictability that it really is. But more than that, they are worried that customers or internal stakeholders will be upset if their project doesn't start right away—you saw the downside to that in Myth #3 – You Have to Run More Projects to Get More Done.

The key to responding to these kinds of challenges is to refocus the discussion on the finish date you are committed to meet instead of when you plan to start working on it. Doing so is much easier when your planning, scheduling, and execution system starts providing improved predictability. After all, haven't you ever asked for a project to be completed earlier than necessary just because you doubted that your supplier would deliver as promised?

What's Next?

This chapter has summarized how a high-performance Innovation OS can regulate project entry based on pipeline bandwidth and avoid derailing the projects you are already running. In the next chapter, I'll explain how to make sure that everyone in your new product organization works to aligned priorities.

Accelerator #5: Synchronize Priorities for Crystal Clear Workflow

A Lever 2 & 3 Strategy—focused on *Doing Projects Better* and *Increasing Resilience*

Now that your project has entered execution, you want it to flow like a relay race—easily and swiftly with a minimum of interruptions. But even if your business is large enough to have dedicated teams for each project, there will still be some resources shared across multiple projects—resources with unique expertise or capital-intensive ones like testing labs or pilot plants.

That means you must synchronize priorities across the organization so that everyone knows what they should be doing today. Otherwise, it's easy for important projects to get hung up waiting for resources. That synchronization is impossible without clear, stable priorities. That means your people need to know the answer to these two questions—and hopefully without a lot of effort.

1.   What should I be working on now?
2.   What should I work on next?

These sound like simple questions—don't they? But in most companies, the answer is anything but crystal clear and stable. Instead, it depends on who you ask.

When projects invariably run into these resource conflicts, most people at the operational level will admit that their company resolves it with the "Wheel Method"—and no, I don't mean a roulette wheel. I mean the squeaky wheel or the big wheel. Whoever makes the most noise or whoever acts like they have the biggest (ahem...) influence gets the resources.

That's when the politicking and infighting begins. These are the same kinds of conflicts that create disharmony as discussed in Accelerator #3 Harmonize Tasks and Role Definitions. They sap engagement and commitment, and most managers get tired of playing referee.

The conventional wisdom that causes much of this conflict is that strategic priorities should drive all priorities—including day-to-day execution. Some project managers learn to manipulate this to their project's advantage—not necessarily what is best for the company.

Probably no surprise, but again I'm going to share an approach that challenges that view. While counterintuitive, using strategic priorities for execution just isn't practical. It creates confusion and can cascade delays across programs. Don't get me wrong. Strategic priorities are critical—most notably in making it crystal clear which projects the company will move into execution when resources from other programs free up. It's just that they are challenging to interpret at the execution level.

Instead, consider splitting priorities into two parts. Strategic priorities determine the next project to come off the backlog. But operational priorities need the clarity of a relay race handoff, so the project that is most at risk of finishing late gets priority access to resources— especially if the goal is an on-time finish. Bear with me through this next example, and any remaining fog around execution priorities should lift.

Project Greenlight is your company's newest program and your highest strategic priority. At the 3-month point, it is 25% complete and looking like it will finish well ahead of the promised launch date. At the same time, Project Yellowlight, your second-highest priority, is looking like it will just barely finish on time one month from now.

That's when you hit a bump in the road. Both projects need the same shared testing resource to complete the next three weeks of work. Following strategic priorities, Project Greenlight gets the help first. Consequently, Project Yellowlight finishes three weeks late and misses the promised due date for an important customer.

So what's the alternative? Suppose instead you prioritize the resources based on the risk of finishing late. In that case, Project Yellowlight gets the help first and finishes just on-time while Greenlight still has plenty of buffer left to assure an on-time finish. A much better outcome all the way around.

Follow this approach, and you'll keep projects flowing more smoothly, have happier clients, and increase new product throughput—i.e., make more money.

The Buffer that Synchronizes

Accelerator #2 Build Resilient Project Plans with Realistic Timelines introduced the buffer as a tool for protecting each project's timeline. It turns out that a project buffer is also an essential tool for synchronizing priorities.

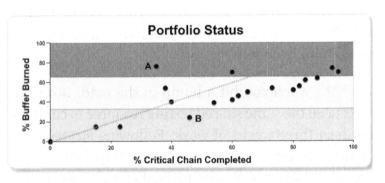

Figure 19 – Portfolio Status Chart

Projects get into trouble when they burn buffer faster than they complete critical chain tasks. Plotting your projects' buffer status alongside the others, as shown in Figure 19, gives you a clear visualization of which projects are getting into trouble and need resource priority.

The vertical axis shows the percentage of buffer burned. The horizontal indicates the fraction of the critical chain completed. The projects residing above the diagonal are burning buffer too fast and more likely to finish late. Don't worry—the Critical Chain Project Management software I recommend graphs this for you in real-time.

This Portfolio Status Chart provides a visual signal that is easy to interpret. If Projects A and B both need the same resource, Project A would be the priority. That's because it has a higher percentage of buffer burned vs. critical chain completion. Priority is not a reward for burning more buffer. It's merely a strategy to increase new product throughput by bringing more projects in on-time.

The portfolio view is a snapshot, but sometimes you need to go a level deeper to see how a project is really doing. That's what you see in Figure 20, where it's clear that this project is blocked and needs attention.

You'll hear more about what actions the project team can take to help get a project back on track in the next chapter.

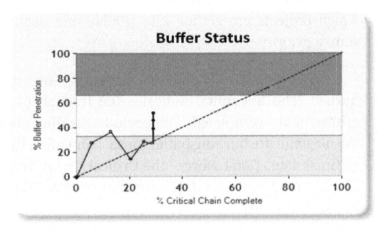

Figure 20 - Buffer Status across Project History

Daily Updating

To have this kind of information available for all your projects, the people working on them need only make one daily update in your project management system. As shown in Figure 21, they simply provide their best estimate of the amount of work remaining for their task. On good days, they will report a decrease. On bad days, they might not make any progress. The key is daily reporting based on the latest information available.

	Task Name	Task Status	Task Manager	Resource Types	Planned Duration	Remaining Duration	Edit Task
cc	Task 18	WIP	Eugene Engenue	Eng(1)	8	6	✎
	Task 19	Not Started	Tim Timmers	Test(1)	3	3	✎
cc	Final Task	Not Started	Matt Matthews	Mfg(1)	5	5	✎

Figure 21 - Updating Days Remaining for a Task

Some folks will push back on daily updating. But it's the only way to have reliable, real-time information on every project. And the entire update process only takes two minutes a day with cloud-based tools and even less with a mobile app.

One exception is longer waiting tasks, such as ordering tooling or waiting for an outside resource to complete market research. Some software tools can automatically countdown these tasks, with the task manager needing only to check in periodically.

When someone marks a task as zero days remaining, it is complete according to the task definition. Then it's time for them to look in their workflow report for the next available task. If there is more than one, they follow execution priority rules to make sure they work on the one most at risk of finishing late.

Benefits of Prioritization

Working in an organization where priorities are crystal clear and stable is significantly less stressful—to be sure. Beyond that, people also view the transparency around priorities as inherently fairer and less political, driving engagement.

This transparency was especially important for an HVAC components client of mine. The climate between product marketing, engineering, and procurement had become highly political. Marketing was driven to bring more new products to market. Procurement was incented to run cost-down projects.

The business needed both types of projects in its portfolio, trapping engineering in the middle. Every project required resources from both groups, but they only wanted to work on those lined up with their incentives. This resulted in constant project meetings to replan as the people doing the work were pulled back and forth, rarely accomplishing planned activities.

Together, we crafted a system that combined balanced governance with clear priorities. Doing so eliminated most project replanning meetings saving thousands of work hours per year, which they redeployed to real work.

Months after rollout, the team achieved better than 90% on-time performance, and the projects that finished late were only a few days late—not the months late that they had been experiencing before. Additionally, employee surveys showed significant improvement in adherence to priorities, workflow, and team communications—and all with a lot less time spent in stressful and frustrating meetings.

Potential Pitfalls

Clear, stable priorities are a powerful guide for any company, but there are a few pitfalls you'll need to avoid.

Pitfall #1 Ignoring Priorities – Some managers will continue to want to set priorities the way they always have—maybe they enjoy the power or want to be able to trade favors. Or perhaps it's because of pressure from somewhere else in the organization. Whatever the reason, it's critical to design your operational meetings and escalation processes in a way that prevents this from undermining continued progress.

Pitfall #2 Inflexible Priorities – There are cases where projects come along that are so strategically important or have such a high cost of a day's delay that you need to act differently. That could be economic opportunity cost or perhaps even liquidated damages. One way to accomplish this is to designate these projects as mission-critical so that everyone knows these projects always get priority access to shared resources.

Your approach must be flexible enough to handle these exceptions without being so relaxed as to invite abuse. Otherwise, people begin to doubt the system's integrity and feel like they can ignore it anytime a "Big Wheel" flexes their muscles.

What's Next?

This chapter has summarized how your Innovation Operating System can help your team prioritize their work and establish a crystal clear workflow. In the next chapter, I'll explain how to visualize flow so that you get an early warning when projects begin to go off track.

Accelerator #6: Get an Early Warning — While You Can Still Recover

A Lever 2 & 3 Strategy—focused on *Doing Projects Better* and *Increasing Resilience*

There's nothing more frustrating than finding out that a project is in trouble when it's too late to do anything about it. Unfortunately, far too many struggling projects go unnoticed until they are well off-track.

It's like piloting a fighter taking off from an aircraft carrier and finding out there is a problem halfway down the runway. At that point, there is precious little distance left to course-correct before you are out of time.

And you know what that means—an all-hands drill to save the project or a fatal crash. Either way, it's a huge distraction that cascades delays by pulling resources off healthy projects and tying you and your managers up in constant meetings to deal with one crisis after another.

The first strategy striking at this issue is a visual early warning, which we'll cover in this chapter. The other strategy is the daily huddle, which we'll cover in the next.

Visualizing Projects Needing Attention

With people reporting daily progress, you can see how each project is doing by simply plotting the % buffered burned vs. the % critical chain completed. Again these charts are something that any good Critical Chain software will be able to provide automatically. The best tools go a step further and factor in performance trends and differences in project duration to provide early warning risk quotients and richer visualizations. They also make daily task updates as easy as using a smartphone app.

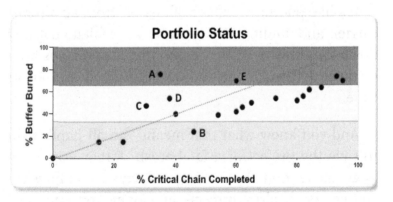

Figure 22 – Portfolio Status

Figure 22 provides a view of every project in the portfolio. Conceptually, the way it works is that anytime a project is above the virtual horizon connecting the lower left and upper right corners, it is burning buffer faster than it is completing work. So Projects A, C, D & E need attention to ensure they stay on track to recover buffer and finish on time.

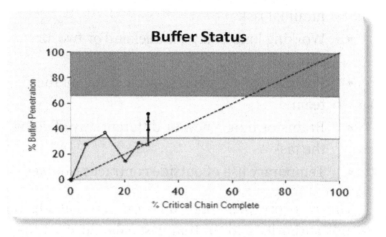

Figure 23 – Buffer Status History of a Project

Going a level deeper into Project C, the buffer status chart in Figure 23 makes it easy to see that a task is blocked because the current task has consumed 20% of the buffer without making any progress. The project manager needs to identify the blocking issue and get the resources or expertise required to resolve it. If the problem is outside the team's scope, they need a clear escalation route.

Recovering Buffer

Recovering buffer may sound complicated, but it merely means figuring out how to complete some critical chain tasks using less time than planned—like the crunching covered in the chapter on planning. Some possibilities include:

- Finding tasks you can work in parallel with minimal risk
- Working longer days, a weekend or two, or overtime
- Borrowing an expert resource from another team
- Brainstorming a new or different way of doing the task
- Temporary use of outside contract resources

The recovery plan may take on risk outside the team's authority and, in that case, should need management approval. One example would be placing an order for long lead time materials earlier than planned. Is the financial risk worth it? If you know the cost of a day's delay before starting any project, you'll know the answer.

A comment on working longer days and weekends—people are often willing to do what's needed if it doesn't become a regular expectation. But prolonged periods of overtime sap engagement and productivity. An early warning system helps break the cycle of crises and fire drills making overtime for buffer recovery more the exception than the rule.

Benefits of Early Warning

Being able to see problems before they derail a project and its on-time finish is a game-changer. When companies start using visualization tools, the problems and issues don't all go away. But because the team now addresses them early and often, they are dealt with before they become crises—again striking at the roots instead of hacking away at the branches.

Potential Pitfalls

While visualizing flow for early warning helps prevent delays, you will need to be careful of these potential obstacles.

Pitfall #1 Customer Delays – Customers expect to work to their timeline—not yours, and that can significantly delay a project if you are not prepared. In some cases, you can avoid that by sharing timelines and updates with customers upfront, so they understand what is required and have ample warning. It's even better if you can break the project into stages with handoff to the customer as the stage deliverable.

When delays like this are unavoidable, design your change control process for rapid assessment of the damage and likelihood of recovery. During this period, customer communications can be delicate and require carefully designed and agreed protocols.

Pitfall #2 Scope Creep – The longer a project takes and the more delays it experiences, the more likely it is that someone will want to change the scope. Getting projects moving quickly and making steady progress against a committed timeline will eliminate most internal scope creep.

But what about external scope creep when doing bespoke development for a single client? Be aware that many large companies train engineers and procurement professionals to convince suppliers that a requirement change isn't really out of scope and that you should accept it with no time or cost impact. Your change control processes must be ready to deal with these situations and cannot treat them casually. The customer and your sales team need to know that you follow a process that evaluates any change to the plan or requirements for cost and schedule impact.

What's Next?

Now that you have an early warning system as part of your Innovation OS, the next chapter shares an essential strategy for mobilizing your team to stay on track.

Accelerator #7: Huddle Daily – Even if You Think You Don't Have Time

*A Lever 2 & 3 Strategy—focused on **Doing Projects Better** and **Increasing Resilience***

The system outlined in the previous chapter provides you with an Early Warning. But then what? It takes people working together with a sense of urgency for the warning to do any good. And that means your people need to meet and communicate frequently.

The problem with most project meetings is that the project team only gets together to review progress every week or two. Or more likely to discuss what did not get done. That's because these meetings often rely on commitments made in a vacuum without considering the other projects vying for the same resources. So a week or two later, they meet and again discuss what didn't get done and make a new plan. Somewhere along the line, it becomes clear the project is running late. That's when the costly fire drills begin.

Communication and a sense of urgency are essential to avoiding crises in execution. And we've all heard people complain about the need for better communication to the point of fatigue. Wouldn't you like to move past talking about it to actually doing something about it?

Believe it or not, striking at the root of this problem only requires a simple fifteen-minute cross-functional meeting. It's not just any meeting, but a unique daily team huddle focused on visualizing the progress each project has made and what is required to maintain the flow.

The initial resistance to these meetings always amuses me. The same people that complain about poor communication can't be bothered to spend 15 minutes of their day communicating. To be fair, their real frustration is that they don't want to spend 15 minutes of their limited time on ineffective communication. And who can blame them?

So the nature of project communication must change. And it can now that you have robust plans, the right number of projects in flight, real information about the project status, and clear, stable priorities available at your fingertips.

The FlowView™ Board [9]

During the daily standup, your teams gather in their work areas in front of a wall-sized board representing the flow and current state of every project moving through your system—what I call the FlowView board.

Based on Agile Kanban principles [10] from the software development world, the FlowView board is a wall-size magnetic whiteboard. It has vertical lanes representing the flow of work and horizontal swim lanes for different workstreams that can go on in parallel. For example, it could have swim lanes for software, electrical and mechanical tasks done simultaneously.

For each project underway, you create a card and place it on the FlowView board. You may need more than one card per project, depending on the number of activities you can run in parallel. It's good practice to label each card with the project identifier and other useful reference information such as the project due date or the customer name. You should also include additional items such as status flags and the current task manager's name.

As resources become available, you pull the cards from a Ready column into a Doing column. Then you move completed cards into a Done column. That becomes a Ready column for the next activity.

For example, in the FlowView board section shown in Figure 24, Project #9 has been through full-kitting. It is now ready for Mechanical Design or Software Development when the assigned resource becomes available.

Full Kit Completed	Mechanical Design	BOM Completed	Place Parts Order	Waiting for Parts
9	7 6	4 5	3	2 1
	Software Development	Ready for Testing	Software Testing	Software Revision
	5 6 7 8	4	3	1 2

Figure 24 - Example Section of FlowView™ Board

When the mechanical design is complete, and the bill of material is in place, the task manager moves it to the BOM Complete column—meaning it is ready to Place Parts Order. The card stays there until someone in purchasing is available to pull it into the Place Parts Order column, and so on.

With the board prominently displayed in the work area, the team and anyone inside the company can easily see where each project is and whether it's blocked.

Previously clients would ask about making the FlowView board digital. However, I believed that digital boards missed the point and discouraged them except with teams spread across physical locations. Digital just couldn't provide the same ever-present, in-your-face visual that forces communication about the things that are keeping your projects from flowing.

However, with the price of large 4K TVs (86-120") having fallen below the cost of magnetic boards, that's changed. Software-based solutions now make sense as that in-your-face visual even for teams working at the same location. Additionally, connecting the digital FlowView board with your CCPM software reduces the work necessary to maintain the board since it can automatically reflect status changes.

If you do go digital, purchase the largest flat-screen TVs available and locate them in central meeting places so that people in each location can easily visualize progress.

There are many software tools available to create and manage boards like this. My recommendations are available at:

<u>GuidedInnovation.com/Software-Choices</u>

The Standup Huddle

The standup huddle occurs in front of the FlowView board and is limited to only 15 minutes. So before the meeting, the leader reviews the buffer status charts to prioritize the projects most in need of attention. That way, during the session, they can focus on the exceptions—the projects where a task is blocked, where your project management system shows you are at risk because a project is burning buffer too quickly, or where a critical handoff or deliverable is approaching.

Working from that priority list, the meeting leader quickly "walks the board," asking the current Task Managers or Project Leaders to report on each project at risk and move any task cards that need to be updated. Some useful questions are:

- What was accomplished yesterday?
- What should be completed by tomorrow?
- Are there any critical handoffs coming up?
- Is anything blocking progress, and if so, what help is needed?
- Do any issues need to be escalated for management's attention or action?

If that sounds like a lot to cover in fifteen minutes, it is. But remember, your priority is the projects at risk. If you don't get to the projects that are doing well at every meeting, it's not a problem because they don't need the same attention.

One of the benefits of sizing tasks between 1-3 days, as covered earlier, is that it helps create both ownership and energy. As the team sees work regularly moving across the board, there's a natural desire to want to be part of the progress. You might even see a little friendly competition and peer pressure to get more done.

But how do you scale this approach across larger, geographically distributed teams and organizations? In these situations, you can subdivide standups into separate meetings among members of a workstream that coordinate and collaborate frequently. For integration purposes, you may also need a follow-up huddle with the leaders from each workstream.

The same approach applies when you have teams distributed geographically. If each region works on a different workstream, you might only need a standup for each, along with less frequent integration meetings. But if your teams share tasks across regions, you need global participation and some way of sharing the board–be that software or video.

Benefits of Daily Huddles

About six months into using this approach, one large manufacturer did an informal survey of their management and leadership teams to identify the benefits. While they had reached 95% on-time performance, what most impressed the management was the sense of urgency and how well people worked together. The weekly, sometimes even daily, crises had all but disappeared. The division marketing and sales VP summed it all up by saying, "We broke the cycle and were able to stop the bleeding and stop the blaming."

Potential Pitfalls

While the daily huddle dramatically improves communication, you still need to be careful of several potential obstacles.

Pitfall #1 Problem Solving – Sometimes, this is tough for technical managers, but if you are going to keep standup huddles brief, you can't let them become problem-solving or strategy meetings. Problem-solving happens after the standup when the project leader and a sub-team meet to plan ways around the obstacle and ways to recover buffer so they can still deliver on time.

With the right software and the FlowView board in place, you can easily see who is working on each task. But when a project is blocked, the standup leader must identify the other necessary resources and make sure they get assigned to solve the problem outside of the meeting.

Pitfall #2 Non-Escalation – There are many reasons a project task can become blocked—technical problems, supplier problems, customer changes, and approvals of all sorts. But to make finishing projects on time more than just lip service, you must have a process that freezes blocked projects and a manager responsible for seeing that they are rapidly escalated and resolved.

People also need to know that non-escalation of an issue to save face is not acceptable. Not only is escalation expected, but there are also no reprisals for raising issues of any sort. People inside your company may doubt this at first, so provide special recognition for the first folks to escalate their issues.

Also, consider recognizing teams that are brave enough to kill hopelessly blocked projects—especially when they do so early. You're not encouraging failure. You are acknowledging realism and how difficult it is for a team to admit that the company should spend the resources on another project.

What's Next?

Now that you have the tools to get execution under control, it's time to talk about what you can do to leverage your new capabilities on better opportunities.

Accelerator #8: Boost Your Pipeline with Better Opportunities

A Lever 1 Strategy—focused on ***Doing Better Projects***—improving the quality of the opportunities you put into your execution pipeline

You're probably wondering, "Why has it been so long since we've seen another Lever 1 Strategy?"

When a company struggles with new product development, they often describe some level of chaos. Sometimes all-out chaos. Sometimes only disorder. But things are never calm and in control.

I've chosen the sequence for presenting and implementing these strategies with an emphasis on alleviating that chaos as quickly as possible.

Alternatively, what would have happened if finding better opportunities had been the first step. Without first freeing up capacity, where would you have gotten the resources to conduct the market discovery work? And how would the people who worked hard to uncover those new opportunities react to seeing them stalled by chaotic execution?

You can see how de-motivating that would be—hardly the kind of situation that helps you build the momentum needed for a sustained transformation.

Instead, getting execution under control first frees up some of the resource capacity you need to do this kind of work. That means you can start to leverage your execution capabilities on **Doing Better Projects**—the fun stuff of leveraging your newly unlocked development capacity and execution capabilities into new and existing market segments to boost your growth.

Getting Out of Your Own Lab

As an experienced business leader, I don't need to tell you that getting into your customer's environment is the best way to find new opportunities. But too often, this responsibility is left to the sales and marketing team.

Not enough companies get their technical people out into the field with any regularity. But when teamed up with capable commercial folks, they have a unique capability that you should be harnessing. Able to view the customer's problems from your technology's perspective, they can connect the dots in a way that commercial folks can't do by themselves. And that's critical if you want to identify new opportunities that your competitors can't.

A Field Guide for Finding Unmet Needs

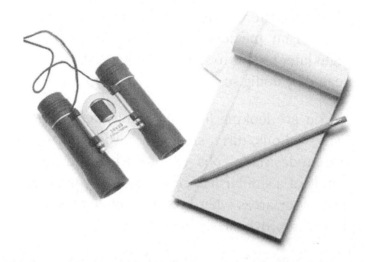

But just sending folks out into the field isn't enough. I'm sure you won't be surprised to hear me say they need to have an objective and a plan. Here are six essential elements to conducting customer field visits in industrial or business-to-business markets – although many of these concepts also apply in consumer markets.

1. Never Enter the Jungle Unprepared

Cross-functional teams, consisting of marketing, technical, manufacturing, and sometimes other functions must prepare before making any visits. They need to develop an interview guide and determine what role each will play in the interview (lead, scribe, clarifier, observer, etc.)

2. Focus on Unmet Needs

Focus customer visits on finding unmet market needs. That includes finding problems that you might later be able to solve and identifying the value created by doing so.

You are looking for the complicated, difficult, costly, tedious, dirty, smelly, hazardous, or otherwise undesirable jobs or obstacles and workarounds of a similar nature. Of course, you are also looking for areas where your technology can simplify or improve the situation.

Think Mary Leakey, the anthropologist, there to unearth facts about a different civilization. Maybe even a little Sherlock Holmes searching for clues. Remember, though; you're there to study the natives in their environment, not change them—at least not yet.

3. Discover Their Limitations

What limitations, restrictions, or problems are apparent in the customer's life–be that in their workplace or home? Here there's no substitute for getting into the customer's world and observing them firsthand.

It's best if you can observe people at work—continually asking them questions to make the assumptions around their practices explicit. That's

where you can most easily identify the limitations—
in the context of actual jobs being done.

4. Dig to Get Below the Surface

You must get below the surface of the problem.
Continue asking why until you get to the root cause.
Then continue to go deeper to find elements of the
problem where you might eventually develop a
profitable solution.

And don't worry if the conversation is uncomfortable. You don't need to feel guilty because you're
there to find the places where you'll eventually be
able to help.

Getting below the surface also requires finding
the right level and function in the organization.
Meetings with purchasing are necessary when selling, but which function has the problems you are
trying to unearth? And are you getting to a high
enough level within it to later influence purchasing
decisions?

5. Look Through a Customer Value Lens™ [9]

New product success in industrial and technology markets depends on helping customers sell
more, spend less, or free up working capital. Your
interview guide needs questions designed to unearth these. Additionally, the interview team needs

to include someone capable of discussing economic issues at a detailed level with clients.

Too often, companies get locked into a mindset that justifying new product programs is all about the financial return they will see—so-called inside-out thinking. This thinking is even more prevalent in financially driven companies with gated processes.

But we all know that customers are only listening to station WIFM—What's In it For Me. So you need a framework that works from the outside-in—what I call the Customer Value Lens:

a. How does removing the limitation make the customer's life better and create value for them? In the case of a business, how does it help them make more money by profitably increasing top-line revenue, decreasing working capital, delaying capital investment, or reducing operating expenses?

b. What is the customer's investment to switch, and what kind of a payback time would they expect? There are always switching costs, even if only the opportunity cost for time spent qualifying your solution. And unless driven by regulation, you rarely find anyone that will switch for a payback period beyond two years.

c. How does the customer's payback translate to a price? It helps to have someone who knows how to think like an economist and use Excel to model the pricing vs. payback.

d. Given that price and your estimated cost, what kind of cash flow would you expect, and is it worth the investment? You've probably noticed that we're back to what's in it for us, but we got there based on an outside-in approach. That's far better than the inside-out cost-plus pricing that leaves so many companies under-performing on margin.

6. Keep Them Talking

The detailed type of information mentioned above is hard to get unless the customer feels you need it to determine if you can develop a win-win solution—develop being the operative word. Any premature solution discussion shuts down the information flow because they suspect you're trying to gather information to put a price tag on the solution.

For that reason, conduct these visits without a salesperson if you can. These are marketing visits, not sales visits, and it can be quite a challenge for some salespeople not to jump to discussing potential solutions prematurely. After all, that's part of how they add value. It's not impossible to include them, but I don't recommend it.

Benefits of Boosting Your Pipeline with a Customer Value Lens

One client implemented this approach to identifying an unmet need for a packaged solution to help drive down energy costs. Initially, they just wanted to sell more of their existing commoditized parts. But using the Customer Value Lens approach, they discovered a market that wasn't focused on component pricing but was interested in a system that could deliver faster payback.

Putting together customized solutions with a short payback period allowed them to quickly develop new business with significantly higher margins than for components alone.

Potential Pitfalls

Pitfall #1 – Missing What They Are Saying– You must listen to what the customer is saying, but sometimes it's just as important to pay attention to how they say it or even the body language they exhibit. The problem is that keeping everything from the interview straight means that you could easily miss essential clues pointing to an opportunity for you to address a profitable new unmet or unarticulated customer need. It requires impeccable listening skills and excellent note-taking.

Interview teams must learn to choreograph these sessions effectively and assign specific roles to capture every nuance. The same is true for the formal debrief following the visit. Plus, if you have scheduled multiple interviews, always debrief before conducting the next interview. It's critical to use what you've learned to improve future sessions.

Pitfall #2 Ignoring Resistance – So you've uncovered an incredible new opportunity with attractive economics. Maybe that looks like all you need to move forward with requirements drafting and then development. But you still need to assess and plan for resistance.

While you can help remove a limitation, the market has lived with that limitation for some time now. That means there are norms, policies, regulations, sales channels, and even institutions that have enabled companies to work around those constraints with alternative approaches. The status quo can create formidable resistance. So can a product that requires reeducating buyers or users. So it's an important step to consider what kind of resistance you might face and how you can reduce that friction to make your solution easier to adopt.

An example of this is a company trying to launch flexible ductwork meant to replace traditional sheet metal in homes and office buildings. They uncovered resistance that would have been very hard to overcome. First, they would have had to change the thinking among general contractors. And even though fireproof, they would have had to convince local authorities to re-write building codes—a monumental undertaking. Finally, they would have seen significant resistance from the sheet metal trade unions.

Even with exceptional labor and material savings, they had to plan to avoid resistance. Knowing that well-established markets would take ages to penetrate, they instead focused on high-growth builders in states and counties without entrenched regulation.

Pitfall #3 Getting Ahead of Yourself – It's important to note that this strategy is only for advanced users. In fact, it's challenging to get here without first putting the other strategy elements solidly in place. That's because you typically need to break the project logjam to make the right technical people available. You'll also need to invest in training to avoid sending your teams out into the wild unprepared.

What's Next?

This chapter summarized tools for finding better opportunities and understanding the potential customer value created. The next chapter will share an approach that helps you build momentum for your New Product OS changes.

Accelerator #9: Structure for Continuous Improvement from the Start

A Lever 1, 2, and 3 Strategy—focused on every aspect of new product innovation.

We've covered a lot together so far. But you might be starting to wonder if this might all be a bit much to undertake. After all, transforming your new product operating system, all the way from ideation to successful launch, can sound daunting.

I'm hoping this strategy may be an eye-opener in that regard.

Decades of experience in uncovering hidden innovation capacity and reaching new levels of on-time predictability has taught me that how you structure and manage your improvement effort is nearly as important as the changes you decide to make.

Change is hard enough without unrealistic expectations. Still, far too many leaders make the mistake of expecting perfection on the initial rollout. Doing so guarantees that the implementation will take far longer than necessary. And that's a grave mistake—sapping critical momentum.

You've seen it—organizations and the people within can get bored quickly—now more than ever. And the longer it takes to see positive results and benefits, the lower the chances are that the change will be sustainable.

Notice that I didn't say "the longer it takes to implement." It takes a year or more for changes to become embedded in your company's culture. [11] The key is in structuring for results early—better performance even if not yet "perfect."

What's more, much of the energy focused on perfection is simply wasted because you won't get it perfect anyway. You are making a change from how you used to work to a new and different way of working. That means unexplored territory for the people in your organization. They can't anticipate every possibility until they start seeing the system in action.

Sure, with the right guidance, you can avoid self-inflicted wounds. But an innovation operating system relies on the coordinated efforts of living, thinking, and feeling people. Even though you can avoid the known pitfalls and plan for the unexpected, people will invariably behave and interact in ways you didn't anticipate.

Moreover, even if you can sustain your initial momentum through a protracted implementation, the naysayers and pessimists will have a field day when the first little problem surfaces. So what's the alternative?

A More Agile Approach to Change Management

Instead, consider structuring your transformation approach so that you get Version 1 of your new product operating system up and running as quickly as possible. Not perfectly, but delivering enough improvement that everyone sees the potential. Good enough for a passing grade.

The first step is to establish a directional goal for the performance you want to achieve longer-term. Then you can determine what metrics you need and set an intermediate target for improvement—where you would like to be in six to twelve months.

Often, managers start out wanting to set ambitious targets along too many dimensions, including on-time performance, new product throughput, and time to market. But it's essential to pick one of these as your guiding light. Most changes will improve all of them, but there are sometimes trade-offs, and knowing which one is the priority heads off a lot of disagreements.

Choose that guiding goal based on a diagnosis of what is constraining your growth. It's also likely to be the issue causing the most stress and drama within your organization. One company that had lost a major customer due to serial new product delays found it relatively easy to agree that honoring their due date commitments should be the guiding goal for their changes.

With your guiding goal and intermediate target established, it is critical to get Version 1 of your new system designed and rolled out quickly so that you can:

- Begin getting real-world feedback on the changes you've made and see what works best in your environment.
- Course-correct early, learn from any mistakes, and continue improving.
- Begin building momentum and quieting those pesky naysayers.

Then once you've rolled out Version 1 and have it up and running with a passing grade, you can begin managing for regular and continuous improvement. Each improved version should focus on bringing your performance up another grade level.

The key here is to structure your implementation for improved results early in the transformation and build from there. That way, you create and sustain momentum, which helps embed the changes more firmly in your culture.

This concept can be a little scary to some. But it might help to view it this way. Your immediate goal is to begin delivering noticeable improvement towards your guiding vision as soon as possible. Reaching that first passing grade is only one of many steps to come in your continuous improvement journey.

After Action Reviews

As part of continuous improvement, it's critical to evaluate the lessons learned during each major project—including each phase in implementing these changes. Often referred to as project post-mortems, I prefer the term that the US military uses—After Action Reviews (AARs). It's a more balanced connotation that doesn't presuppose that you can only learn from failure.

To conduct an AAR, gather the project team and answer these questions:

1. What did the project charter and plan say was supposed to happen?
2. What actually happened?
3. What worked well that you'd like to build on for future projects?
4. What would you like to improve?
5. Were there any unanticipated obstacles that we should factor into upcoming plans?
6. Are there any projects running where we can put what we learned to use right away?

Dashboard for Continued Improvement

A key benefit of using CCPM software is that the automation makes many of the strategies already covered much easier to implement and sustain. But another important element is the rich array of data that you can use to drive further improvement. See my recommendation at GuidedInnovation.com/Software-Choices.

At the simplest level, your organization gets valuable feedback on how they are doing relative to improvement goals for on-time performance and project throughput. But having this data also enables more sophisticated dashboards; product, project, and portfolio managers can then drill down into the data to drive targeted improvement.

Figure 25 is a screenshot of a Pareto or 80/20 analysis of the reasons for delays. In this case, the SDL Reason Code, Supplier Delivered Late, is among the top three contributors to delays. Instead of spreading improvement across the entire system, this dashboard allows you to focus your efforts on the few issues that create 80% of the delays. The result is far more impact from your constrained resources.

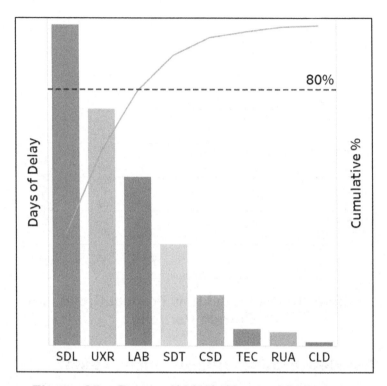

Figure 25 – Pareto (80/20) Chart of Delays by Reason Code

You can also link data from your CCPM software with CRM forecasts and ERP data to view expected and actual results for the portfolio. Figure 26 shows the growth anticipated from current programs in the portfolio. This picture tells you that additional opportunities are needed to continue driving increases in new product growth past Year 3.

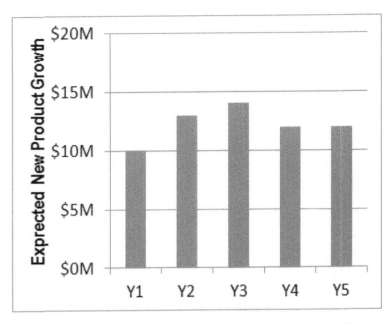

**Figure 26 – Expected New Product Growth for
Current Portfolio**

The New Product Improvement Team

The real value of AAR's and the Dashboard is in putting what you learn to use. That's the role of the New Product Improvement Team (NPIT). The NPIT brings together managers and influencers from across all the departments involved in bringing new products from idea to reality. During monthly meetings, this team reviews performance metrics and learnings from across the organization and decides how to apply them to do more with your constrained resources. They also review progress on the small handful of active improvement initiatives and curate and prioritize the backlog of NPIT initiatives awaiting resources.

Aligning Organizational Structures and Performance Management Systems

Another element of continuous improvement is aligning your organizational structure and the goals, objectives, and other parts of your performance management systems with the transformation you are leading.

Involve your human resource team and ask people in each department what they see as the internal obstacles that could trip up improvement. It's also helpful to list the goals and measures for each group and look for misalignments that could cause problems.

You also need to evaluate whether your organizational structure might be creating conflicting goals and incentives. This often happens in matrix organizations if metrics don't link functional contribution to top-level business goals.

Earlier, I mentioned the engineering group caught between corporate marketing and procurement. The matrix environment rewarded procurement for driving down costs and marketing for increasing sales of new products. Without shared goals, the procurement group leader directed his people to prioritize cost-down projects over new products. A cost-down focus was helpful in highly competitive segments. However, it was a significant distraction in growth segments where the company needed to accelerate new product launches.

Misalignments like this are something you need to identify and deal with early. But they will still creep back in over time. Your New Product Improvement Team needs to identify these issues and act on or escalate them as they emerge.

Potential Pitfalls

Now that you've seen a more agile approach to change management and eventual transformation, here are a few pitfalls your leadership team will want to avoid.

Pitfall #1 Winging It – Structuring for continuous improvement isn't the same as trial and error—trying something and then if that doesn't work, trying something else.

As the Hippocratic Oath goes, "First Do No Harm." So before beginning the change process, you need to identify proven building blocks that will take you to a better place than where you are today. The strategies I've shared so far should point you in the right direction.

Pitfall #2 Not Casting a Wider Net – True continuous improvement involves everyone in the enterprise, and people want to know how they can contribute. So invite involvement from anyone with ideas that can drive faster or more predictable new product execution. Ideas that help the organization get more out of its constrained resources. Then prioritize those ideas as part of the New Product Improvement Team initiatives. You can also cast a wider net by inviting interested folks to attend monthly listening sessions at the beginning of each month's New Product Improvement Team Meeting.

Pitfall #3 Not Celebrating Enough—Remember, people love to be part of a winning team. So communicate and celebrate early and on-time finishes. Celebrate improvements in your metrics. Celebrate new initiatives. Even consider celebrating when you kill a project because those resources can now go to a better purpose.

Pitfall #4 The Rearview Mirror Problem - Once you roll out V1 of your innovation operating system and see some immediate improvements, it's easy to make the mistake of taking your foot off the accelerator and coasting. After all, your team has been driving hard to get the new system in place, and you've just put yourselves ahead of most other companies.

But remember—the competitors in your rearview mirror are closer than they appear. The improvements you've made will give you some breathing room. But don't make the mistake of thinking your competition isn't doing everything they can to improve their capabilities—be that shortening development lead times, finding exciting new opportunities, or simply getting new products to market on-time.

> **"The competitors in your rearview mirror are closer than they appear "**

You don't want to become a sitting duck for those competitors. Instead, you want to remain a moving target that is accelerating and increasing your lead.

Pitfall #5 Failing to Leverage – I wrote this book for business leaders, and the best have a clear vision for where they want to take their organizations. Where could you take your company with this kind of performance?

Imagine for a moment that you have overcome the status quo and transformed your new product innovation operating system. You can now develop more new products in less time and with a higher level of predictability than any of your competitors.

What kind of competitive advantage could you turn that into—especially in highly engineered environments?

Remember, you had to overcome conventional thinking to get here. You've made changes that your competitors don't understand and aren't likely to attempt. What would happen if you now started leveraging the fastest, most predictable product development capabilities in your industry?

And once you prove that you can deliver on your promises, what if you attached an on-time guarantee—putting your money where your mouth is, as they say?

That may not fit your business model; regardless, it's still worth spending some time strategizing how you will leverage these new capabilities.

What's Next?

This chapter summarized the importance of a learning and continuous improvement approach for your Innovation OS. The next chapter will talk about the kinds of improvements you should expect.

No Silver Bullets

Theory of Constraints (TOC) and Critical Chain Project Management (CCPM) are two cornerstones of my strategies—because they work, and when used correctly, deliver rapid and sustainable results.

Though I've shared examples throughout this book, there is a significant amount of published information on other companies' achievements. A study of more than 60 Critical Chain implementations among many well-known organizations reported the following results: [12]

- Higher than 90% on-time completion
- 39% reduction in equivalent project duration
- 70% more projects completed
- 53% more value delivered from those projects

These results beg the question, why hasn't every company moved in this direction?

Unfortunately, too many managers are looking for a silver bullet. And while the accelerators shared here can create dramatic improvements, they still require significant organizational change and transformation. Or, to paraphrase Edison, they come dressed in coveralls and look like work.

Your Innovation Operating System is part of your company's DNA. As harmful as they can be, conventional project and resource management practices have rooted themselves in that DNA; it takes a concerted effort to eradicate those roots. Think about the number of times your organization has made changes that you were excited about only to see them erode and fizzle out over time—delivering far less than you had hoped. That's the status quo at work, especially if your changes are only hacking at the branches.

Significant and sustained improvement requires a solution that strikes directly at the roots of the problem. But it also requires a proven roadmap for change. And that's exactly what I designed the Guided Innovation Operating System to be.

What's Next?

You've just seen the magnitude of the improvement that's possible. You also know that you need to prepare for the change effort required. These final pages will prepare you for some of the obstacles you might run into so that you can make plans to avoid them.

Obstacles You Should Expect

Imagine for a moment what it would be like to have a high-performance Innovation OS that enables you to move past the finger-pointing and silos. What would it be like to put the delays behind you and regularly launch high-impact new products on-time without the drama? Picture your new product teams fully committed to delivering critical programs faster than your competitors and being energized and excited about the future. That's an advantage any leader would want.

Hopefully, you've gained some insights into how you can achieve that kind of advantage by unlocking your company's innovation productivity. But as I've done throughout this book, I'll again share some of the obstacles or pitfalls to avoid as you begin putting your high-performance operating system in place.

Potential Pitfalls

Pitfall #1 Being Afraid to Lead Change – If you've read this far, you've probably decided to act on what you've learned. However, I've seen some managers bury their heads in the sand and try to ignore or downplay innovation issues. As you can imagine, that never ends well.

The improvements within their grasp should have energized them. Instead, they were afraid to shine a light on any of their challenges. As if not talking about the problem meant it didn't exist. At the core of it, they were afraid of how exposing the problems would reflect on them.

Transparency like this can be especially tough for some New Product Development or R&D leaders who often take much of the blame for these problems. Sometimes unfairly because innovation is a team sport, and many of the resources involved in new product projects are simply outside of their control.

The key here is leadership. Change is, after all, a leadership activity. And you can still choose to lead even if you don't have the final decision. It's about turning that reflection around and owning the problem. Taking a stand for what you know is best for the company and ultimately for everyone within. It's time to get out ahead of the issues and lead your organization to buy into a better way.

Pitfall #2 Getting Buy-In Backward – Too often, managers get buy-in backward. In their enthusiasm and zeal for a better way, they lead with the solution. Then they are surprised by the pushback and skepticism. With all the reasons that "It won't work here." Some even give up and become bitter because "No one here ever wants to change."

High influence leaders learn to overcome this by leading people to the change instead of leading with the change. They know that people aren't naturally resistant to change—only to change that makes them feel insecure or that they think is being pushed with a hidden agenda.

Start by building a consensus that the problem exists and it is worth solving or that a higher level of excellence is achievable. You might notice that I didn't start this book by talking about the Nine Proven Accelerators and their benefits; I started with the problems and the root causes.

That's an important model and why the first step in my implementation roadmap focuses on identifying the current system's undesirable effects. You can't win the hearts and minds necessary to move beyond the status quo when you lead with the solution. Instead, you need to surface the problems and the opportunity costs broadly so that managers and influencers across the organization have the space to reflect on them.

If you want others to buy-in, you must, as Covey put it, "First, seek to understand." [13] As a good leader, you can probably list most of the problems without asking anyone else. But that is beside the point. They need to know that you listened and feel that you understood their concerns and views. Being heard is essential before they truly trust your direction instead of just nodding yes without any real agreement.

Pitfall #3 Failing to Quantify the Problem – What is predictable new product growth worth to your company? As an example, let's say your current new product vitality (percentage of sales from new products) is 15% and your goal is to reach 25% over the next three years. With a variable margin of 50%, the 3-year cash flow impact is equal to $10 million for every $100 million in total revenue. If your revenue is $50 million today, that's $5 million. If your revenue is a billion, that's $100 million.

Pitfall #4 Going It Alone – It's easy to think you can fix this yourself, especially if you are worried about exposing problems. The problem with that lack of transparency is that it can turn those silos you want to eliminate into hardened bunkers.

Innovation leaders are fast learners. They often feel, "Once I've read the book, I know what to do." But as the saying goes, "The Map is Not the Territory." And making sustainable changes within organizations of any size is unquestionably complex. When results matter, there's no substitute for working directly together with an experienced advisor—one that has done it dozens of times and has the proven roadmap to take you and your organization through the journey quickly and effectively.

After all, there is a cost for every day of delay. What is the cost of taking a year or two to see results? Shouldn't your goal be to get your improved Innovation

OS in place and accelerating results as soon as possible? The roadmap we use gets you there in as little as 90 days.

Still, some will choose to go it alone, thinking it less costly. But if the value of rapidly achieving that added cash flow and market share doesn't dwarf the cost of getting help, should change even be a priority?

What's Next?

You've learned a lot in the preceding chapters. What you get out of it depends on you and what you do with what you've learned. Carefully follow these proven strategies, and you will see gains.

But if you'd like to find out how you can accelerate those gains, you might consider our no-fee, Innovation Operating System Roadmap Session on Page 147 or visit:

GuidedInnovation.com/Roadmap

About the Author

Mike Dalton founded Guided Innovation Group to help businesses that depend on new product growth uncover their hidden capacity.

During a 24-year career within the $10 Billion SC Johnson & Son family of companies, he developed unique expertise in applying constraints-based methodologies to new product innovation. Since then, he's worked with executive teams across a wide range of industries to expand and leverage this powerful approach.

He frequently speaks at industry conferences and wrote *Simplifying Innovation*, the first book applying Theory of Constraints to new product innovation, and has had numerous articles published in Industry Week, CFO Magazine, and Research Technology Management.

Now in *Unlocking Innovation Productivity*, he offers that experience as a high-performance Innovation Operating System that can help transform your organization—once and for all—to deliver both profitable **and** predictable new product growth.

Bibliography

1 "There are a thousand hacking at the branches of evil to one who is striking at the root." Henry David Thoreau, *"Walden, or Life in the Woods"*

2 Theory of Constraints (TOC) is a powerful focusing framework for all continuous improvement efforts. You can read more about it in Eli Goldratt's seminal work *The Goal*, 1984, North River Press or in my previous book *"Simplifying Innovation*, 2010, Flywheel Effect Publishing

3 Wheelright and Clark, *Revolutionizing Product Development*, 1992, Free Press

4 Ogawa and Ketner, *Benchmarking Product Development*, 1997, Telephony Online, Penton Media.

5 Dalton, *Simplifying Innovation: Doubling speed to market and new product profits—with your existing resources*, 2010, Flywheel Effect Publishing

6 Goldratt, *Critical Chain*, 1997, North River Press

7 Goldratt, *Engines of Disharmony*, 2011, Goldratt Consulting

8 Reinertsen, *The Principles of Product Development Flow*, 2009, Celeritas Publishing

9 FlowView and Customer Value Lens are trademarks of Guided Innovation Group, LLC

10 Anderson, *Kanban: Successful Evolutionary Change for Your Technology Business*, 2010, Blue Hole Press

11 Kotter, *Leading Change*, 1996, Harvard Business Press

12 Kendall and Austin; *Advanced Multi-Project Management*, 2013, J. Ross Publishing

13 Covey; *The Seven Habits of Highly Successful People, 1989*, Simon & Schuster

Keynote Speaking at Your Company Meeting or Industry Conference

How many speakers have you heard that get the audience to question and change their fundamental assumptions on innovation? And in a fun and engaging way?

If you are looking for a speaker to shake up your next meeting, call us at +1(262)672-2700 or send an email to info@guidedinnovation.com

Innovation OS Roadmap Session for Readers

I hope that these insights have helped you build a foundation for improvement with powerful strategies that strike at the root issues you face.

Are you ready to get your company off the treadmill and begin accelerating your improvement efforts? If so, I'm happy to offer you my *Guided Innovation Operating System Roadmap Session* at no-fee.

In this tightly focused session, we'll unpack your new product improvement goals and the challenges standing in your way—all in a no-pressure, no-pitch environment. If you feel there's a fit, we can discuss a roadmap for getting your business moving in a confidence-inspiring new direction. And if you don't, you'll still take away valuable insights for your business.

To schedule your session, contact Mike at:

 MDalton@GuidedInnovation.com

📞 +1(262)672-2700

 GuidedInnovation.com/Roadmap

What Leaders Are Saying About Dalton's First Book

Simplifying Innovation

"Dalton's innovative approach can help any company find the 80/20 spike needed to drive new product growth."
--Richard Koch, bestselling author of *The 80/20 Principle*

" Worth waiting for. Simplifying Innovation synthesizes innovation best practices and the focusing step framework to create a powerful new TOC application. Let it stimulate your imagination as it did mine."
--H. William Dettmer, author of *Strategic Navigation*

"Now that's innovative - a business book that's entertaining too. The powerful lessons that Dalton shares inside are like jet fuel for companies that want to propel their growth."
--Ed Petkus, VP - New Products & Engineering, Hawker-Beechcraft Aviation

Available in Print, Kindle, and Audiobook formats

Made in the USA
Middletown, DE
01 March 2023

26008253R00089